THE ISRAELI–PALESTINIAN PEACE PROCESS

OSLO AND THE LESSONS OF FAILURE
Perspectives, Predicaments and Prospects

GW00975974

Studies in Peace Politics in the Middle East

Volumes 1 and 2 are published in association with the University of Oklahoma Press

The Israeli–Palestinian Peace Process

Oslo and the Lessons of Failure

PERSPECTIVES, PREDICAMENTS AND PROSPECTS

ROBERT L. ROTHSTEIN, MOSHE MA'OZ AND
KHALIL SHIKAKI

sussex
ACADEMIC
PRESS

BRIGHTON • PORTLAND

Preface, Introduction and Conclusion, and Editorial Arrangement,
Copyright © Robert L. Rothstein 2002

The right of Robert L. Rothstein, Moshe Ma'oz and Khalil Shikaki to be identified as
editors of this work has been asserted in accordance with the Copyright,
Designs and Patents Act 1988.

2 4 6 8 10 9 7 5 3 1

First published in hardcover 2002; published in paperback 2004 in Great Britain by
SUSSEX ACADEMIC PRESS
PO Box 2950
Brighton BN2 5SP

and in the United States of America by
SUSSEX ACADEMIC PRESS
920 NE 58th Ave   Suite 300
Portland, Oregon 97213–3786

All rights reserved. Except for the quotation of short passages for the purposes of
criticism and review, no part of this publication may be reproduced, stored in a
retrieval system, or transmitted, in any form or by any means, electronic,
mechanical, photocopying, recording or otherwise, without the prior
permission of the publisher.

British Library Cataloguing in Publication Data
A CIP catalogue record for this book is available from the British Library.

Library of Congress Cataloging-in-Publication Data has been applied for.

Paperback ISBN 1-84519-058-0

Typeset and designed by G&G Editorial, Brighton
Printed by Antony Rowe Ltd, Chippenham, Wilts
This book is printed on acid-free paper.

Contents

―――――

―――――

Contents

Preface

The chapters in this book were prepared for a conference held at Colgate University in late March 2001. More than nine months have elapsed since the conference, nine months in which momentous events have occurred. Any book about an evolving international issue, such as the Oslo peace process, runs the severe risk of becoming irrelevant or "overtaken by events" before it appears in print. This seems especially true when the intervening developments have been as shattering as the brutal terrorists assaults of September 11, 2001, and the continued and accelerated "race to the bottom" in the Israel–Palestinian relationship. Nevertheless, however grim the prospects may now seem, since there is no alternative (or no better alternative) to the resumption of peace talks at some point in the months ahead, I would submit that the developments of the past nine months have made the effort to understand the Oslo process even more crucial and the lessons that we have attempted to extract even more (potentially) useful to future negotiations. Providing evidence for this argument necessarily means that this Preface is also a Postscript.

I want to comment here, if very tentatively, about three post-conference developments that have affected or may affect the future of the Oslo peace process: first, a venture into "second-track" diplomacy that emanated directly from the conference; second, the effects of September 11th on the political dynamics of the Israeli–Palestinian relationship; and third, the effects of the escalation of Palestinian terrorism, especially the suicide bombings in Jerusalem and Haifa on December 1st and 2nd, on the peace process. One hardly needs to add that, as I write on December 6th, the after-effects of these terrorist actions remain unclear. Optimists might argue (or hope) that the worldwide condemnation of these attacks might finally induce Arafat to act against terrorism and Sharon to retaliate judiciously, but optimists are an endangered species in the Middle East.

As frequently happens at conferences, what goes on out of the public eye (in the corridors or on social occasions) may be as important as what goes on when papers are formally presented. That was true in the Colgate conference circumstance. In private conversations some of us came to two conclusions. The first was that, despite many disagreements, there were surprising elements of agreement or near agreement on some of the most controversial issues left unresolved at Oslo or Camp David II or Taba (at the end of the Clinton administration). Private positions seemed more flexible and more amenable to compromise than anything either side was prepared to say publicly, at least before the resumption of formal negotiations. This suggested that a venture into "second-track" diplomacy – a private, semi-official negotiation between a small group of well-connected individuals – might be useful. Such diplomacy became possible because of the generosity and vision of Colgate's Dean and Provost who quickly offered to support our venture.

Our second conclusion was that since this was not going to be an academic conference and since we needed participants who had access to top decision-makers and who were also committed to a negotiated settlement, we needed to revise the list of participants. In the end, five of the nine participants (including this writer as a "facilitator") were from the original conference and our four new participants are very well-known political and military figures. The willingness of these individuals to participate is testimony to the fact that thoughtful people are very aware that continued deterioration of the peace process could be disastrous for both sides and that efforts have to be made to achieve a cease-fire and to reach mutually bearable compromises on the very tough final status issues that remain unresolved.

Our meeting was held in July. I cannot reveal the names of the participants or the terms of the documents that we produced, in part because our efforts have not entirely ceased and in part because some of the participants strongly prefer anonymity. But I do want to say something about our efforts in general because I believe they reveal something about both the limits and the possibilities of second-track diplomacy.

We had, in discussing our agenda for the July talks, felt that both sides would have agreed to or been compelled to accept a cease-fire at some point in the ensuing three months. Thus it was our original intent to concentrate on two of the key final status issues that had generated so much conflict at Camp David II and Taba: Jerusalem and the right of return for Palestinian refugees. In the event our optimism about a cease-fire proved sadly naive, the violence continued and even escalated, and we were forced to refocus our efforts on the terms of a deal that might generate a real commitment on both sides to ending the violence and resuming the negotiating process.

Our talks were initially tense and confrontational but gradually the outline of a potentially important joint statement began to emerge. We took as our baseline the recently published Mitchell Report, since both sides had made ostensible commitments to implement it, but we felt that we could strengthen it by removing some of the ambiguities and by being more precise about who should do what and when. Perhaps even more importantly, we felt that a joint statement involving *major* substantive concessions by both sides that was signed by figures of such eminence – individuals who were well known in both camps and who were not identified and discounted as the usual "peaceniks" – might galvanize the moribund peace process. Apart from the debate that would have been generated by the statement, we also felt that the reputation of the irreproachable signees of both sides would provide cover for Mr Arafat and Mr Sharon to make the concessions they were unable or unwilling to make on their own.

Unfortunately, our effort floundered at the very last minute because one of the key Palestinian participants decided, after a night's sleep, that he could not sign the statement because of the commitment to take very strong action against terrorism. There is some irony in the fact that after September 11th Arafat was compelled to accept even stronger anti-terrorist actions, but too late to be very convincing. There were indeed risks in signing not only for this participant but also for Mr Arafat because the use of violence had become so popular in the Palestinian community (and well beyond the extremist movements), and because no other strategy seemed likely to achieve the maximalist gains that Mr Arafat apparently felt he had to achieve. This episode may also have revealed one of the hidden costs of inviting participants to a second-track negotiation that are *too* well-connected: they may find it more difficult to take positions that are unpopular at home or that stray too far from a previously articulated stance. Still, an opportunity to move back toward the negotiating table may have been lost, as all the participants subsequently recognized. It may also be worth noting that subsequent official efforts to restore the peace process were actually more modest in aim than what we almost achieved in the summer of 2001, if unofficially.

Second-track diplomacy can be both intensely frustrating and intensely exciting. The private and informal nature of the talks permits possibilities to be explored that would be impossible in an official setting where the fear of appearing weak inhibits a willingness to move away from fixed positions. In any case, what this participant found most valuable – and also most maddening – about our discussions was that they revealed that reasonable men on both sides were far closer to an agreement on the issues than the public debate might suggest. But when leaders are too weak or too fearful to make compromises that meet the minimal substantive needs of the other side, second-track diplomacy cannot move the game forward. This does not mean that it is useless: it does create a small network of influential people on both sides who are aware of new possibilities, who can communicate these publicly or privately at home, and who have a better sense that the "other" is more diverse than first appears. This may help to diminish the ever-present fear that the other side is not really prepared to negotiate seriously and will renege on all commitments.

The peace process continued to deteriorate during the summer months and there was no obvious way out, especially with a new administration in Washington that was not willing to risk much political capital on restarting it. In effect, the Bush administration's foreign policy team seemed more interested in proving how different from Bill Clinton they were than in working to resolve one of the world's most critical conflicts. To give them their due, however, the risks of engagement were high (as were the risks of non-engagement as became quickly apparent), and peacemaking with reluctant peacemakers was, and is, notoriously difficult, indeed perhaps impossible without very strong external pressure. Leaders who use the peace process as a different way to carry on the conflict or to score political points at home or abroad (seeming tough for home consumption, seeming moderate and flexible for external audiences) cannot sustain the momentum behind a fragile peace process. Both leaders had also backed themselves into a bargaining corner by establishing prerequisites for the resumption of negotiations that would involve great risks for the other. Testing the credibility of the other by posing questions that the other – as one knew – could not answer was not sensible unless the whole effort was an elaborate charade to ensure that the other was blamed for the failure of the peace process. Or perhaps this is merely another way of saying that peace processes are popular because they bring status, resources and time, but that peace agreements, which require both sides to make difficult concessions, are an entirely different matter.

The horrendous assault on the World Trade Towers and the Pentagon on September 11th by Osama bin Laden's Islamic terrorists created a genuine "day of infamy," the full implications of which are still unclear. The United States (and its friends and allies) certainly learned how vulnerable they are to terrorists who are willing to sacrifice their lives in order to instill fear and destabilize Western societies in the name of some paranoid – if not psychotic – fantasies disguised as "Islamic." And the fears have escalated as we contemplate even small groups of terrorists armed with chemical, biological and nuclear weapons. The United States – and Israel with it – have also been shocked at the hatred that has been vented against them by hysterical mobs of Islamic extremists in a variety of countries, ostensibly because of US military assaults against the Taliban and bin Laden's Al-Qaeda terrorists and US support for Israel. On one level, these events have made many commentators aware of the need to fight terrorism by a variety of means in a variety of places – because the victims are no longer just "elsewhere" – but, on another level, they have made many begin to question (as yet quietly) the wisdom of supporting authoritarian regimes in the Middle East that style themselves as friends and as supporters of Israeli–Palestinian peace but meanwhile quietly support terrorist groups, ruthlessly repress freedom in their own countries, and fill their controlled media with the most vile anti-Semitism and anti-Americanism. With friends like these . . .

The events of September 11th and their aftermath also had, and will continue to have, a profound effect on the disintegrating Israeli–Palestinian peace process, although the effects (at least at the time of writing, December 2001) are partially contradictory and may end once the Taliban and Al-Qaeda have been defeated. After all, short of compelling the Israelis and the Palestinians to accept an imposed settlement, which some on both sides have begun to advocate out of a sense of desperation, the constraints and conditions that have made peacemaking so difficult have escalated sharply in the last few years; gaps between the two sides have widened and frustrations, resentments, and grievances are growing deeper and more entrenched. Needless to say, neither leader has made any effort to educate his people for peace – Arafat has in fact done quite the opposite – and it seems unlikely in any case that many could hear or be willing to listen as the bombs explode. Moreover, an imposed peace could become a recipe for disaster since neither side might be fully committed to a peace they had not created (and thus did not "own"). Furthermore, the willingness of the United States to stay the course with sustained political, military and financial support is always contingent on the next change in administration or the shape of the new systemic crisis. New leaders in the two communities might also help to sustain the peace, especially as Arafat's credibility and support continue to erode, but there is hardly a guarantee that they will be an improvement on the incumbents. Put differently, Arafat is the worst of all leaders, except for the alternatives, and Netanyahu – if he returns to power – could make Sharon look like a moderate.

In short, pessimism about the short-term prospects for Israeli–Palestinian peace is surely warranted. Still, there were a few *small* signs that burying the peace process might be premature, although the terrorist attacks on December 1st and 2nd, the Israeli reaction, and the potential for civil war within the Palestinian communities if Arafat finally does act seriously against the terrorists he no longer seems able to control, may extinguish even these signs that the door to peace has not been slammed shut. In any event, we ought at least to make note of these signs.

In the first place, the United States has been forced back into the peace process because of the need to keep the coalition against the Taliban and Osama bin Laden together: Muslim allies have demanded movement on the Palestinian–Israeli front in order to diminish protests in the "street" against support for the United States and its allies. It is, of course, far from clear that even a successful peace process between the Israelis and the

Palestinians will diminish the wave of protests because brutal, corrupt and incompetent regimes will not suddenly become democratic, responsive and prosperous because of a peace agreement that is bound to leave many on both sides unhappy and willing to go on fighting. Ironically, the autocratic regimes may in fact be most at risk if they lose the ability to use Israel as a rationalization of repression and ineptitude.

Whatever the long-term consequences, the short-term effects of a more active role by the United States, signaled by Secretary of State Powell's address of November 19th, are as yet unclear. But the potentially beneficial effects are great because progress without a strong US role is unlikely. In any case, the coalition against the Taliban and Al-Qaeda seems to be holding together reasonably well, although this may be due more to the apparent rout of the enemy forces than to the US diplomatic initiative. If the war drags on and the Taliban and Al-Qaeda succeed in launching a guerrilla war, and Osama bin Laden evades capture or death, strains on the coalition are inevitable. Nevertheless, for the moment, the return of the US to the peace process in the Middle East may be the catalyst necessary to restart the peace process. But it takes three to tango, so to speak, and success is likely only if one can also foresee changes in policies and perspectives by Arafat and Sharon.

Are there any signs that the failure of the peace process and the events of September 11th have generated a degree of learning in both communities and their leaderships? No clear and simple answer is possible because the peace process has become a prisoner of events – the next terrorist incident, potential leadership changes, a new international shock, whatever. The initial reaction of Arafat and some part of his community to the events of September was radically different: while large numbers of the Palestinian citizenry was reported to be dancing in the streets, joyful at the death and pain inflicted upon thousands of innocent Americans and others, Arafat – presumably having learned from his incredible blunder in rushing to support Saddam Hussein's brutal invasion of another Arab country – ordered his security forces to crush any further demonstrations of support for the terrorist assault and tried to align the Palestinian movement as rapidly as possible behind the anti-terrorist campaign. This kept the Palestinians in the game as possible beneficiaries of US pressure to restart the peace process.

These benefits presupposed, however, that Arafat could or would make a genuine effort to stop Palestinian terrorism and arrest and punish any individual or group that refused to desist. Arafat had made many promises to do so in the past but had always broken those promises, presumably because the use of violence was popular and efforts to stop it could be risky. Doubts had also grown that Arafat, a product of his past, was neither capable of nor willing to accept a compromise settlement – except perhaps as a stage to launch demands against Israel itself. Thus the credibility of his promises either with the Israelis or the Americans was nil. What was potentially different now was that worldwide condemnation of terrorism was much stronger. These two factors gave Arafat a degree of leverage to crack down on terrorism and to make the case to his own people that suicide bombers could not bring peace. The terrorist strategy had surely inflicted pain on Israelis and greatly increased psychic insecurity about daily living, but is joy at inflicting pain worth the cost of very high numbers of Palestinian deaths, increasingly impoverished standards of living, children on the street rather than in the schools, the virtual destruction of the Israeli peace movement, and the disintegration of a peace process that nearly brought the Palestinians a relatively good settlement at the end of the Clinton administration – a settlement that may no longer be available? Arafat's response to that question has never been satisfactory but the intense pressure that has been put on him after the terrorist attacks of December 1st and 2nd may finally compel him to act – or perhaps, conversely, as is his usual style, to promise anything and to deliver only more promises.

Unfortunately, Arafat is caught on the horns of an agonizing dilemma. As terrorist assaults lead to increasingly severe Israeli reactions, death and destruction mounts and so do the demands for increased compensation to make it seem as if the deaths were meaningful and heroic. Caught between his own people's support for the continued use of violence and their opposition to action against the extremist groups and the demands of Israel and the United States to take strong action immediately to stop additional terrorist assaults, he has no safe options. Why risk a civil war to get to a bargaining table that might not have much on it? The likely response, if the past is a guide, is that he will hedge and waffle and dodge and divert in the hope that something will turn up to eliminate the need to do anything drastic. The notion that this time – finally – faced with threats to his survival from both Hamas and Israel, Arafat will have no choice but to act decisively is superficially appealing but may yet again run aground against familiar obstacles: the lack of alternative leadership, the fear of civil war, Arafat's skill as a survivor. The US initiative is thus not likely to get very far unless the pressure on Arafat is intensified (say, by a cutoff of US and European financial support) and unless Israel is willing to offer him some concession (say, on settlements) to justify taking a big risk for peace – something that Israel does not yet appear willing to do.

(The latest twist in the plot, after the above was written, was the sudden announcement by Hamas and Islamic Jihad that they were suspending – not ceasing – terrorist activities, presumably to avoid civil war, and in response to Arafat's pleas. This is a rather typical Arafat tactic to deflect pressure and to avoid the necessity of actually destroying the terrorist networks, but it is hardly likely to satisfy the Israelis who know that terrorism will return when the pressure is lowered.)

Israel, conversely, initially reacted to September 11th on the basis that it now had free rein to go after the Palestinian terrorist network as if it were an outpost of Bin Laden's Al-Qaeda. The Israeli response to continuous terrorist actions had been relatively restrained – at least in Israeli eyes – because the military had not attacked in force and because the targeted but extra-judicial killing of known terrorists was not very different from President Bush's call to get Osama "dead or alive" or Bush's willingness to suspend or threaten various civil liberties in order to make it easier to pursue and prosecute terrorists.

Israel soon discovered, however, that what the United States could or would do was not what Israel could or would do. The imperatives of keeping the coalition together against the Taliban and Al-Qaeda, and thus restarting the peace process, prevailed over the feeling of Sharon and many Israelis that their terrorist threat was structurally similar and justified similarly severe responses to Palestinian terrorism. Sharon was publicly rebuked and the President and the Secretary of State broke new ground in talking openly about the West Bank and Gaza as occupied territories and the creation of a Palestinian state. In short, the retaliation against Al-Qaeda's terrorism did not give Israel carte blanche against the Palestinian terrorist networks, but the outrage of December 1st and 2nd may have created a new dynamic. The latter atrocities occurred just after an American mission arrived to try and move the peace process back on track – an all too direct and insulting response by the terrorists. But the mission surely must continue for there is no sensible alternative to a cease-fire and the resumption of negotiations which might restore some hope to the Palestinians that a renewed peace process just might produce widespread gains (and not merely for Arafat's coterie), and to the Israelis that living a normal life will become possible once again. Terrorism for terrorism's sake, merely to enjoy inflicting pain on the other, is unlikely to bring the Palestinians nearer to any of their (reasonable) goals; and more force and more targeted assassinations by the Israelis succeed only in keeping a losing game going.

Finally, another dynamic in Israeli public opinion may also justify a degree of hope. The outpouring of hatred against Israel from the Arab (and Muslim) "street" and the demand by the fundamentalists for the destruction of Israel increases doubts in Israel that a genuine peace would ever be possible or that the Arab world would ever accept a Jewish, democratic and prosperous Israel as a legitimate Middle Eastern state. From this perspective, any concessions to the Palestinians would simply be used as a platform to make new demands until Israel itself was at risk. Arafat's maximalist demands at Camp David and his popularity for rejecting a very generous offer by Clinton and Barak seemed to confirm this ominous view of Palestinian intentions. Still, Israeli intentions have evolved. A recent poll (reported by J. J. Goldberg in *The International Herald Tribune*, November 30, 2001, p. 6) found 55 percent of Israelis still saying Israel's best option was an accelerated effort to make peace and only 20 percent favoring an intensified war against the Palestinians. A substantial minority of Israelis (44 percent) even favored the idea of a peace imposed on both sides by the United States. This suggests there is more room for a serious effort at peace-making than might at first seem evident, but the opportunity may be lost – again – despite or perhaps because of Arafat's weakness, his demanding too much too soon, or his loss of control, a leader without followers. If any or all of these possibilities prove true, the peace process may be doomed until new leadership emerges, perhaps in both countries.

*   *   *

It would take a very brave or a very foolish person to make a strong prediction about the near term course of events, let alone anything long-term. We have become prisoners of events and prisoners of our anxieties, an extraordinary accomplishment for an evil fanatic in control of a relatively small group of men willing to die as a complex expression of their hatred for the West, the United States, Israel and the Jews, and Muslims who do not share their vision of Islam or the evils of the modern world. Whatever happens to Osama bin Laden and his key collaborators in the present conflict, enough of these people seem likely to survive, to pursue the acquisition of the most destructive weapons, and to remain intent on killing as many "enemies of Islam" as they can. This presumably implies that the terrorist threat will be the defining security threat for at least the next few years or longer. It also seems likely to mean that the conflict within the Islamic world is likely to escalate, a conflict not only between two different versions of Islam but also between the brutal reactionary regimes still in power in the Middle East and the forces of democracy and modernization that are desperately seeking to emerge and triumph.

The peace process between the Israelis and the Palestinians has been buffeted by the turmoil generated by the events of September 11th and their aftermath. But that peace process also runs on its own track, and local and regional developments are likely to remain more powerful and consequential than events elsewhere, which is not to deny the importance of the latter. And it is a peace process too important on its own terms to become a residual of policy needs elsewhere in place or time. It is also too important to be left as a residual of the play of domestic politics, as has been true in both camps for more than a year. The struggle of old war horses to stay in power, helped by the ability to blame the other for everything, has come to dominate the need to break out of the inherited constraints of the past.

Pessimists and realists always seem to win the battles in the Middle East but the war still goes on. I have suggested that a small and perhaps fleeting window of opportunity may have opened for progress in the peace process because of the interaction of a number of factors: the return of the US as an active player, perhaps some rethinking of the utility and wisdom of a terrorist strategy, perhaps some willingness on the part of thoughtful elites on both sides to rethink what peace will require and what it might bring, and perhaps simple battle fatigue in (parts of) both camps. But the window of opportunity can quickly shut because the men of violence can drag everybody down with them and because no one has learned to trust the possibility of peace – to "give peace a chance", as that old cliché goes.

If the conflict continues to escalate, the race to the bottom may culminate in an all-out war that kills many and settles nothing. But the imminence of catastrophe may finally shock even weak leaders, fearful followers, and uncertain external supporters to look for a different route. It is my hope that if and when the peace process is resurrected, the chapters that follow will provide the peacemakers with some important lessons about what to do and not to do to deepen a peace that will be fragile and at risk for years to come.

Acknowledgments

The Conference at which these papers were presented was held at Colgate University in late March 2001. There would have been no conference without the strong intellectual and financial support of Jane Pinchin, then Colgate's Dean and Provost and now Acting President. Jane also offered extraordinary financial and moral support for an ensuing venture into "second-track" diplomacy, which I shall briefly discuss in the Preface. All of us who participated in the conference are very grateful for Jane's support. I also want to thank my colleague Professor Steve Kepnes for the many intellectual and practical contributions he made to the Conference.

RLR
London, December 2001

1

A Fragile Peace: Could a "Race to the Bottom" Have Been Avoided?

Robert L. Rothstein

The Oslo peace process is near death and even its most fervent supporters have almost lost all hope. The "race to the bottom" began almost immediately after the famous handshake on the White House lawn (September 1993) but the pace of deterioration reached near warp speed after Ariel Sharon's infamous visit to the *al-Haram al-Sharif* / Temple Mount. It was a match thrown on a smoldering fire. The opposition to the Oslo Accords, which has been widespread from the beginning, has been more than happy to insist that failure was inevitable: the Israeli right (both secular and religious) because it felt too much had been given away, and the Palestinian left and the Islamic fundamentalists because not enough had been gained (or guaranteed in the future) to justify entering an uncertain peace process. The opposition hardened and deepened as the peace process lost momentum and staggered from crisis to crisis for a variety of reasons: the continuation of pervasive mistrust, the continual failure to meet deadlines, the failure to improve standards of living for the Palestinian people, the dismal and disappointing performance of Mr. Arafat's Palestinian Authority, the petty harassments and humiliations imposed by heavy-handed Israeli soldiers and police – the list could go on.[1] A dismal process produced a dismal outcome, perhaps a paradigm of how not to run a peace process.

This seems to imply that Oslo was a "bad" peace, a peace that was bound to disappoint expectations, or that could not be effectively implemented, or that demanded a degree of compliance that asked too much too soon from one or both parties, or that one or both parties signed only to get breathing space to rearm or to increase external support, or that was forced upon the parties by an external patron with its own agenda. Since a peace with any or all of these characteristics may increase the probability of a return to violence and may make it even more difficult for the next attempt

to jump start a peace process to work, and since any or all of these accusations have been made against Oslo, a bad peace might seem an apt
description.

This argument, however, seems misleading and insufficiently contextual.
There are surely differences in quality between different peace agreements
and some may be more equitable than others or more closely approximate
the minimally acceptable terms of agreement for both sides. Nevertheless,
all peace agreements that attempt to start the process of resolving
protracted and sometimes existential conflicts are inevitably flawed,
fragile, and incomplete. Such agreements should not be criticized for failing
to do the impossible or failing to more fully approximate either side's ideal
notion of what should or can be done. No preliminary peace agreement –
or exploratory truce, perhaps more accurately – in this context is going to
meet all the demands or needs of both parties or clarify and resolve the
central symbolic and substantive issues that have driven and continue to
drive the conflict. And no peace agreement should be called "bad" for only
beginning and not completing the process of making peace or for only
creating new opportunities not new guarantees. Note here that the point is
not merely that such peace processes are bound to be fraught and difficult
but rather that the peace processes themselves are going to be affected in
fundamental ways by the characteristics of the conflict and the way in
which it has evolved (a point to which we will return in detail below).

In short, such agreements are largely blank canvases or canvases with
only a few faint lines drawn in. What happens next awaits the skill and
imagination of the painters/peacemakers. Only a victor's peace could
promise more and, apart from the fact that neither side has conceded
defeat, such a peace may only create more long-run problems than it
resolves. Moreover, the alternatives offered by the naysayers are hardly
superior: we are now witnessing a return to violence, to the desire to inflict
pain on the other even if the inevitable retaliation is even more painful, a
"politics of the last atrocity."[2]

The argument thus far necessarily implies that the standards we should
use in evaluating Oslo and other such agreements must be as tentative,
provisional, and open-ended as the agreements themselves. We can really
know whether Oslo is good or bad only after some time has passed and we
can assess how well our painters/peacemakers have implemented the agreement, taken advantage of opportunities to deepen it, and understood the
need for new patterns of thought and action in the post-peace period. This
period, rather like the period after a new democratic government has been
established, has both dangerous continuities with the past and new opportunities that can be grasped or ignored. Ignoring either the continuities or
the opportunities can turn a protracted conflict into an insoluble one.

The limiting case argument here is something of a paraphrase of

2

Churchill's famous comment on democracy: Oslo is no one's idea of a good peace, except for the alternatives. Oslo was a product of its times, a period when both sides for different reasons were willing to explore the possibility of a new relationship but were also still distrustful and suspicious, not in full control of their domestic constituencies, not fully convinced that painful compromises were necessary or wise, ever ready to interpret the failings of the other as a justification for using the peace as a new means of carrying on the old conflict, and unwilling to risk much or to gamble on a high risk/high gain strategy. Indeed, in light of prevalent beliefs and attitudes and in light of how much was left unresolved by Oslo – nearly everything of substance – ambivalence and caution were rational and prudent.

The disastrous deterioration of the Oslo process has generated a search for scapegoats: the "usual suspects" include Arafat for the Israelis (and many US officials), Netanyahu, Barak and Sharon for the Palestinians, and Bill Clinton for some on both sides.[3] The burden of my argument is that we need to get beyond scapegoating to ask why leaders felt the need to act as they have. When we get to this level, we will find that a large part of the answer lies in the nature of the peace process in protracted conflicts. Still, while the task of transforming an exploratory truce into a genuine peace process was and is bound to be tense and difficult, the descent did not have to be as profound and bitter as it has become. Individual leadership does make a difference: context is important but not solely determinative. Thus a profound failure of leadership on both sides has made a bad situation worse and turned a peace process into a tragedy. And the hope that such leaders will at least learn from their mistakes seems entirely illusory – as yet.

I want in the rest of this chapter to discuss a number of inferences that can be drawn about the kind of peace process that we can expect to emerge during a protracted conflict. Before doing so, however, it is necessary a few brief comments about the general characteristics of protracted conflict.

Protracted Conflict: Existential Fears, Distrust, and the Absence of Empathy

The costs of protracted conflict are devastating, from brutal and unending violence to the perversion of civic values, psychological traumas, profound economic losses, and the shame of pariah status or the sorrows of a life on the run in exile. Why, then, with elites and publics – if not the "hard men" with the guns and bombs – increasingly desperate to find a way out and increasingly affected by battle fatigue and a sense of the futility of more of the same, has it been so difficult to negotiate compromise settlements more bearable than an ugly status quo.[4] And even an ugly status quo may seem preferable to relinquishing deeply held and sometimes theologically ordained maximalist goals of victory, even victory in the far-off future – however bad the present, it is impossible to disprove the belief that victory by a "long war" strategy of attrition is possible.[5] Moreover, the limited offers that weak leaders can make to each other and the uncertainty that such offers will be implemented or produce enough benefits quickly mean that what can be offered and what can be gotten seem insufficient. Thus it seems more prudent to complain bitterly about the status quo but to risk little to change it. Each side, ever distrustful, fears that compromise offers will lead only to new demands or to an appearance of weakness. There is something akin to what economists used to call a low level equilibrium trap or a bad status quo without any obvious exit option.

Protracted conflicts develop other, deeper characteristics that help to explain why it is so difficult to embark on a peace process. I will only briefly list some of these characteristics because my primary focus is on how – taken as a whole – they affect the negotiating process, not on the characteristics themselves. Thus a conflict syndrome, or a set of long-lasting structural conditions, emerges that sustains and intensifies the conflict: economic inequalities, the isolation of the warring communities from each other, an indifference to learning about an "other" who is to be destroyed, the misuse of history for entirely partisan purposes, the feeling on both sides that they are embattled minorities, and the development of a "conflictive ethos" that fuels animosities, demonizes the other, and strengthens each group's sense of identity and separateness.[6] At some point, after an exchange of atrocities and a hardening of views, such conflicts may become existential: each feels that its very existence is at stake and that any or all means are justified to destroy the other before being destroyed.[7] It hardly surprises that empathy is absent in these circumstances, a factor of some consequence because empathy is the basis of most moral judgments and its absence may also impede the process of learning about the other.[8]

One result of the creation of a deep-seated conflict syndrome is that something akin to a prisoner's dilemma game develops: distrust is so pervasive and the lack of information about the other is so profound that sub-optimal outcomes are inevitable – they are expected and not an aberration. The trick may be to avoid turning a prisoner's dilemma game into a totally irrational game of chicken, of bluffing with lives at stake, which may describe the latest stage of the Oslo process. Another consequence is that "normal" conflicts of interest become more difficult to resolve because they can be transformed into conflicts of symbol and icon that cannot be compromised. In any case, since most peace negotiations focus on compromising the issues on the negotiating agenda, and not on dealing with the subjective or long-run issues that are part of the underlying conflict syndrome, there may be a bad fit between what gets discussed and perhaps resolved during the peace negotiations and the conflictual factors that persist and may – if not dealt with as rapidly as possible – undermine the peace process itself or its aftermath. It is a staple of conflict analysis to argue that both levels of conflict must be dealt with but it is not sufficiently stressed that the long-run issues must be confronted and dealt with from the start to strengthen the constituency for peace, to provide evidence of good intentions to the masses, and to provide immediate, tangible benefits that people do not want to lose.

The very fact that the conflict is protracted and that neither side can achieve some of its central aims or defeat the other side also usually means that both leaders have been weakened (threatened by extremists who promise more and denounce the possibility of a compromise agreement) and that a kind of Gresham's Law of conflict operates with extremists driving out or eliminating moderates. Leaders begin to focus narrowly on staying in power and containing extremists at the expense of exploring a substantive compromise with the enemy. At a minimum, this implies that any peace process that emerges will be tentative, that posturing for domestic constituencies to prove that the leader is not giving away too much and that he is bargaining hard to achieve maximal gains will dominate, and that the process will be slow, crisis-driven, and always in danger of destruction.[9]

At the height of the conflict, in its most existential phases, pessimism abounds and the conviction grows that "no solution is immediately practical."[10] This view is too stark because some movement or some improvement in current conditions is always possible – even between bitter enemies; not everyone is always a "true believer" in apocalyptic visions of the conflict, and taking the "no solution" view too literally may miss important changes that are occurring in both communities.[11] Still, when the conflict is at its most intense stage, suggestions of compromise are likely to seem treasonable, opposition to compromise may be the only position that can maintain domestic unity, the stakes of the conflict seem so high that it becomes an article of faith that the other is completely untrustworthy and always seeking to do the worst, and thus constant demands for quick and strong evidence that any tentative explorations of compromise by the other side are meant seriously are prevalent.

At some point, when both sides realize that they have reached a military stalemate, when the costs of going on seem to weigh more than the ever-receding potential benefits of victory in the "long war," and when the simple desire to begin living a "normal" life becomes increasingly attractive, a "window of opportunity" may open to begin exploring the possibility of peace.[12] This changes the terms of the conflict, opens new opportunities for movement, and may even begin to reorient some cognitive maps but it is obviously a long way from a genuine peace settlement that resolves substantive issues.[13] The road ahead is perilous in large part because the initial agreement and subsequent agreements are largely procedural, because they are not self-executing and terms are constantly exposed to divergent interpretations, the persistence of old attitudes means that the post-peace period will have many continuities with the pre-peace period, and the extremists will be energized to destroy an already fragile peace. In short, the period after a weak peace agreement has been negotiated is potentially transformational or potentially regressive: the conflict can return (as in the Middle East now) or the peace can be slowly strengthened. The key factors in determining which outcome will ensue are likely to be joint efforts to reduce the negative effects of the structures of conflict that still persist and joint efforts to establish new patterns of thought, new styles of interaction, and new cooperative institutions more appropriate for peaceful coexistence.[14] None of these efforts were seriously attempted in the Oslo years and instead each side signaled the other that the conflict was still on – and thus generated a negative self-fulfilling prophecy that quickly came to pass.

I want now to discuss what the foregoing arguments imply about what we should expect or anticipate from any peace process that does begin.

Fragile Peace and the Management of Expectations

There follows **six** conceptual points about what we can reasonably expect from very fragile peace processes.

1 As I have already suggested, we cannot expect that either side will make a full commitment to the peace process because initial offers are likely to be minimal, doubts about the other's willingness or ability to offer more or to implement promises will be great, there will be widespread (and not unreasonable) fear about either's ability to get a substantive agreement through domestic political processes, and both will be unhappy about the terms of any agreement and constantly seeking to push its limits or renegotiate its terms. Since these fears and doubts are rational, given the context discussed earlier, reluctant and tentative commitment to a low risk/low gain strategy is intrinsic to the end game of a protracted conflict. Generosity will be limited, demands to dot every "i" and cross every "t" will be pervasive, and haggling over every inch of territory or every symbolic concession will be nasty. Risk aversion will be high because fear of failure will be high and leaders will seek to protect themselves against these risks (to themselves and to the peace process, in that order) rather than to increase the chances of success by altering attitudes and patterns of behavior. In short, there is a

strong likelihood that the temporary truce will revert quickly to renewed conflict because each seeks to manipulate the peace process to gain more or to be stronger at the next stage – faith in the possibility of real peace is too weak to expect much more than a defensive posture.

Perhaps one lesson of this is to avoid the (premature) euphoria that is generated by ceremonies on the White House lawn or grand statements about the establishment of "peace in our time." Expectations are obviously easier to manage if they are not blown out of proportion. This point is worth special emphasis if only because the peace process is shadowed by the ineradicable risk that any apparent shift toward peace is merely tactical, a platform to raise new demands or to achieve ancient goals by slower and at least momentarily less violent means. The fear of being duped is especially strong in the early stages because distrust is still pervasive and the consequences of being wrong about the intentions of the other could be catastrophic for both leaders and followers. These suspicions explain why demands for strong, tangible, and early indications of a serious commit-ment to peace are inevitable – but also dangerous when the other leader is weak, confronts dangerous rivals, and has an insecure domestic base.[15] In any case, the potential conflict between what each leader needs to do to bolster domestic support and to increase his own willingness to run risks and what he needs to do to convince the other side that the peace process is genuine and that momentum needs to be maintained is severe. The results can be disastrous if either or both leaders are unaware of or indifferent to these concerns-which in the case of Arafat and Netanyahu led to the joint conviction that the other was not serious about peace.[17]

2 The second point follows from the first but is frequently ignored, especially by commentators intent on blaming a convenient scapegoat for the latest disaster in the peace process. The point is that the stop/go, off/on, crisis-driven negotiating process that developed after Oslo (and after the Good Friday agreement in Northern Ireland) is not simply the result of flawed leaders and unpredictable political events. This kind of process is not an aberration but rather intrinsic in this context: we can bemoan but we should not be surprised that leaders won't risk more – there is no clear reason whey they should – or that they act with mental reservations, implicit doubts, and a readiness to pull back quickly. We should anticipate a peace process that loses momentum and can easily become a prisoner of events, that is dominated by last-minute decisions on the edge of an abyss, and that moves – forward and backwards – in an erratic and inconsistent fashion.[18] There is a willingness to explore but with an escape hatch to the comforts of the familiar – and leaps of faith into a brave new world are likely to seem bearable risks only to strong leaders very sure of their domestic base.[19]

leaders can only hedge their bets, move slowly, and be excessively
_ic about what benefits can be expected (and how soon) from any
_ive agreement, one needs to understand that such behavior is intrinsic
_is kind of peace process. In effect, it is neither an aberration, nor irra-
onal, nor the result simply of weak and ambivalent leaders. I do *not* mean
to exculpate such leaders: as with Arafat and Netanyahu, they can make a
bad situation much worse, they can fail to adopt new patterns of behavior,
and they can accelerate the race to the bottom. Nevertheless, understood
contextually, we can better understand why they act as they do, why asking
them to risk more or to take actions that threaten their basic power positions is unlikely to work and why other leaders should be careful not "to
set them an exam that they can't pass."[20]

*   *   *

On one level, the first two points might seem another way of making a
simple point: the peace process that seeks to end a protracted conflict will
be fraught. The points are still worth making, however, because they are so
frequently forgotten by leaders overcome by premature euphoria (or by
weak leaders who must promise too much to doubtful followers) and by
external supporters intent on disengaging as rapidly as possible. On
another level, the points have even greater significance. It is at least
arguable that the most important task that leaders confront in the aftermath of the initial agreement is the management of expectations. If the
latter are too euphoric, if hopes have risen unrealistically, a rapid descent
into despair and disillusionment is inevitable. This can easily destroy the
peace process because it will become impossible to build a wider
constituency for peace, the top/down elite-driven peace process will not
begin to generate grassroots support, and momentum will rapidly dissi-
pate. Negative outcomes are especially likely when the lack of empathy
means that one or both sides is unaware of, or indifferent to, what the other
needs.[21] Each side can well end by sending the signal that the conflict
continues, peace is a sideshow. Thus the presentation of the peace process
– the way we "frame" it and set out what can be the expected from it – is
not an exercise in public relations but is rather a major factor in determining whether it will succeed or fail.

3 The third point is to some extent implicit in the first two but it also
begins to lead us into a crucial issue: the domestic politics of peacemaking.
In conventional, interest-based conflicts the most important level of interaction is usually between the parties themselves as they engage in a process
of concession/convergence. However, in the conflicts that concern us here
it is usually two other levels that dominate. Because there is so much doubt
about the commitment of the other side and so much fear of being duped,

leaders (especially leaders weakened by past failures or unstable domestic coalitions) are likely to focus primarily on not getting too far ahead of a domestic constituency that may still believe in promises of ultimate victory or in a demonic view of the other.[22]

Weak leaders may also view the third level of interaction with actual or potential external patrons as more critical than face-to-face negotiations with the old enemy. Thus Arafat might have signed the Oslo agreement not because of any substantive gains – which were minimal – but because it meant that he and the PLO were recognized as the legitimate representatives of the Palestinian people and he might gain status and resources from a new access to the White House. And he might have been reluctant to compromise at Camp David II for fear of negative reactions from the Arab world. On the Israeli side, there has not only been an obvious reluctance to alienate the United States but also a reluctance to use its military power fully for fear of losing moral legitimacy among other democratic states.

The key point here, details apart, is that the most essential bargaining level – face-to-face with the enemy – may become a residual of the other levels and almost epiphenomenal to other bargaining games that are important, but not as important as the face-to-face game. Perhaps another way of making the point is to note that the game is not just about ratifying an agreement between two parties but is also a rolling, multidimensional effort to keep the game going – managing crises, building support, monitoring compliance – that requires all three levels to work together or at least not at cross purposes.

The argument here suggests that the peace process is really a three-level bargaining game. If the interactive effects of two-level games are complex and indeterminate, how much more so are three-level games?[23] Whatever the answer, one thing should be clear. Awareness that the other leader may be posturing for the domestic audience or for the support of external patrons means that there is added uncertainty and distrust at the face-to-face level: how committed can the other be if he seems more focused on different bargaining arenas?

4 The domestic politics of peace is so important that it requires separate treatment. But, given the increasing tendency to argue that domestic politics is always dominant (especially in international political economy), one needs to emphasize that the argument here is more differentiated.[24] Domestic constraints and opportunities can obviously be critical but it seems to me that most leaders involved in peace processes make their choices based on a complex assessment of potential support or opposition on all three levels – not to mention their cognitive biases, the history of the conflict, and their sense of whether or not time is on their side. Out of this conceptual maze – which might make any choice seem extremely risky, including procrastinating – I would guess that the dominant form of decision-making is likely to be a form of "negative satisficing." In short, the leader will make a last-minute decision, fudged as much as possible, that offends the least number of actors who have the power to do him harm.[25]

One needs also to note that the phrase "domestic politics" can mean many different things in many different contexts. One obvious point to keep in mind is that the domestic politics of a democratic state like Israel and the internal politics of a rebel group are very different things, apart from the generic notion that each leader needs to secure his domestic base. Thus the leadership of the rebel group may get its legitimacy from its image of militancy for the cause, not from a free vote, and the notion of a "loyal opposition" is unacceptable because the rebel group values (and needs) unity above all else. In any case, in what follows I do not seek to discuss all the analytical complexities of the notion of domestic politics but rather only to highlight certain aspects that are relevant to the peace process in protracted conflicts.

Oslo was a top/down peace, driven by elite calculations and perceptions.[26] An elite consensus on the need to try the peace track, even if the two elite groups do so for different reasons, may be a necessary first step to break through a stalemate. But at some point the peace process must be broadened and deepened so that grassroots support grows. This complex process has only recently begun to be analyzed in depth but it is clear that it is multidimensional: for example, quick improvements in standards of living, the creation of new institutions to foster cooperation, and longer term efforts to change attitudes, perceptions, and behavior.[27] This process failed dismally after Oslo as neither Arafat nor Netanyahu made much effort to educate their constituencies about the sacrifices necessary for peace or the need to think and act differently in the post-peace period. As a result, as conditions deteriorated the masses began to see the peace as increasing dangers and decreasing standards of living. The pressure from below that did emerge was largely negative: to be tougher, to offer less, to retaliate harshly.[28] The "peace process" became a dangerous farce and its supporters began to abandon ship.[29] Perhaps even worse, because the capacity to make credible promises is an important component of any bargaining relationship, the fact that Arafat had lost total credibility with the Israelis – he had lied too often – and various Israeli leaders had lost credibility with the Palestinians (even Barak who went far toward meeting their demands) meant that the peace process might not be resurrected until new leaders emerged.[30]

Why did the Oslo process deteriorate so rapidly and so profoundly? Peace was never going to be easy but it was not inevitable that the difficult would become the disastrous. One *part* of the answer is that two weak leaders cannot make a strong peace. A leader in a very fragile peace process must accomplish two tasks: first, he must create, sustain and enlarge his domestic constituency for peace; and second, he needs to understand and act on the knowledge that his fate and the fate of the other leader are linked together – to borrow a phrase, they will hang together or hang separately. The leader who can only hide behind his extremists (and even urge them on as Arafat has done in supporting the use of violence after Sharon's visit to the Temple Mount/*al-Haram al-Sharif*) fails in the first task. A leader with no empathy for, or understanding of, the other side or the requirements of a peace process fails in the second task.[31]

A crucial problem that weak leaders face is that internal unity is likely to crumble as a peace process develops and the possibility of controversial and painful compromises suddenly becomes real. The masses, still committed to ancient rhetoric about ultimate victory and perhaps unaware of all the factors pushing toward peace, may well slow the process down and threaten the leadership with severe sanctions. Other elites may also threaten the leader by denouncing compromise and maneuvering to be in a good position if a succession crisis arises. A weak leader, caught between rising domestic opposition and an offer that seems inadequate may see his only choice as negotiating by exchanging atrocities, which may generate internal unity but at the cost of destroying the peace party on the other side – not to mention the rising death toll on both sides.[32]

One tactic that weak leaders can try is to give any group powerful enough to undermine a compromise agreement a seat at the bargaining table (both internally to develop a consensus and externally when negotiating with the other side). It is not clear that this is wise since it gives the outriders a potential veto over the negotiating process or at least the ability to delay it dangerously. In South Africa, where the ANC and the National Party were the dominant players, analysts and practitioners developed the idea of "sufficient consensus" to isolate and control extremists but to allow them also to join the consensus should they decide to accept its premises.[33] But where each side is more divided and the extremists are relatively more powerful, it may not be possible to construct such a consensus – except behind the continuation of the conflict and the rejection of compromise. In such circumstances, the best option may be to create a "coalition of the willing," isolate the extremists, and seek support from the other side to help contain violence and limit the cycle of retaliation. In effect, the "sufficient consensus" may have to cross boundaries.

Perhaps we can get a better sense of the consequences of weak leadership if we briefly comment on the domestic constraints on Prime Minister Barak and Chairman Arafat. Both were weakened by the growing disillusionment with the peace process, although they reacted to this situation in a completely different fashion. The dismal performance of Arafat's Palestinian Authority obviously meant that his popular support declined, that he was fearful of making any of the concessions necessary for peace, that he felt threatened by and thus impelled to undermine an emerging trend toward democratization in the Palestinian community, and that he encouraged the use of violence to bring him what diplomacy could not.[34] It is undoubted this record that led Dennis Ross, the US negotiator in the Middle East, to say of Arafat that "I have come to the conclusion that he is not capable of negotiating an end to the conflict because what is required of him is something he is not able to do. It's simply not in him to go the extra yard."[35] This criticism may be well-founded but it needs to be leavened by an awareness of Arafat's domestic weakness and by an awareness that *all* the choices he faced were risky and unclear.

Barak, in contrast, reacted to domestic weakness in almost exactly opposite terms. While initially strongly supported, his support began to evaporate as the extent of the concessions he was prepared to offer Arafat became clear, as Arafat seemed to increase his demands with each concession, and as Arafat ultimately turned to violence to elicit further concessions. The Israeli public seemed to offer majority support for the peace process but that support was thin because most of that majority did not believe that Oslo would in fact bring real peace.[36] Thus support was neither widespread nor stable. And as violence intensified so did pressures from below, but not for more concessions but rather for fewer concessions and increased toughness. In effect, the domestic risks of peacemaking obviously grew as Oslo produced increased violence, increased insecurity, and increased demands.[37] Perversely, Arafat's tactics seemed designed to destroy a potential partner for peace and to guarantee the return to power of a much harder opponent. Barak responded to declining support for the peace process and for himself by staking everything on a gamble for a "final" settlement at Camp David. When this was rejected by Arafat (and might have been rejected by the Israeli public in a referendum), Barak himself paid a high political price for getting too far ahead of his own constituency or not producing results to justify his risk-taking.[38]

5 The argument that I have made necessarily implies that it is a dangerous illusion to argue that the kind of peace or peace process described will produce "peace in our time" or a quick and easy "normalization" of a relationship that has been dominated by total distrust and deep and unresolved grievances. Thus the kind of rhetoric that President Clinton and Prime Minister Barak used to describe the failed efforts at Camp David II was not only naive but also guaranteed to raise expectations that were bound to disappoint. Dreams of the perfect may harm the possibility of the "merely" good.

Perhaps we can get a better sense of the dangers of raising expectations if we think about the peace process in terms of three levels that are not easily synchronized. The initial level – say, Oslo in 1993 and 1994 – frequently involves a crucial trade-off: an end to violence (at least temporarily and by most combatants) in exchange for recognition of each other as legitimate and necessary bargaining partners. This is crucial, particularly in terms of potential, because it changes the terms of the conflict (what each now might consider) and opens new opportunities for movement. But it is obviously a long way from a genuine peace settlement because few substantive issues have been resolved, the process of implementation of even minimalist terms is likely to be erratic and uncertain, and the number on each side genuinely committed to the process is likely to be small and mostly among the elite.[39] It is at this level that the management of expectations may be most crucial not only because they have probably escalated with the signing of an agreement but also because disappointed expectations can destroy an already fragile peace.

The second level usually involves an important and potentially forcing agreement on how to begin bargaining on substantive issues and some sort of explicit timetable to avoid deliberate delays and compel movement away from extreme demands. One hopes during this period for both substantive progress on key issues and an effort to isolate extremists and to show the masses that there are real benefits from peace that they do not want to lose. Perhaps also some joint institutions can be created that widen the constituency for peace and begin to show some of the beneficial possibilities implicit in mutual cooperation. Presumably expectations and achievements should begin to converge at this stage – at least if some improvements have occurred. It suffices to say that Oslo was an unmitigated disaster at this level.

The third level is more long-term in intent and focus. Given the failures at the second level, this level never became operational but this hardly means it is inconsequential. Since many of the structural problems that have driven and deepened the conflict over the years still persist – even if the peace process has reached substantive agreement – the process of reconciliation can hardly have begun.[40] The problems that remain are thus deep-seated, they will not disappear because a "scrap of paper" has been signed, and it may take decades before success at this level can be achieved. Nevertheless, even if reconciliation can only be built brick by brick through an accumulation of small actions that show mutual respect, a commitment to equity, and a willingness to atone for and apologize for the atrocities of the past, it remains true that efforts need to commence at once. The leaders on both sides obviously never gave this level the slightest thought and began running backwards as rapidly as possible. Expectations that the relationship would begin to change and that each would value the benefits of peace were completely thwarted.

One result was that leaders lost any credibility they might have had (or built up) with the other side. Since the ability to make credible promises is essential for an effective bargaining relationship, and since this no longer seems possible with the present leadership, we confront the grim reality that peace may have to be put on hold. However, the necessity of constructing and maintaining a stable coalition against terrorism after September 11 may finally have forced the Bush administration in November 2002 to make its first serious venture in Middle East peacemaking, with results that are as yet unclear. Finally, one should note that the ultimate aim at this level is not the elimination of conflicts of interest, an obvious impossibility, but rather a commitment to resolve all disputes peacefully and by political means. That this is now utopian should not be an excuse for wallowing in cynicism or insisting "nothing can be done." Some small steps of progress are always possible, indeed necessary, even at the darkest moments.[41]

6 The violence and hatred that have virtually destroyed the peace process in the last six months (since Ariel Sharon's infamous visit to the Temple Mount in September 2000) have had one potentially salutary effect. Both sides have learned, at an unnecessarily high cost, that current strategies are not working.[42] They have not, however, learned how to improve their performances and thus far we have seen only tactical maneuvering and not new strategies. In effect, we have evidence of a negative learning curve: the worse things get, the worse each side behaves. According to one analyst, for learning to occur a sense of urgency, of feasibility, and of desirability must converge. Only the first has spread widely among the elite communities on both sides, which implies that the deeper assumptions about the relationship are unlikely to be changed but that tactical shifts are possible – and at least potentially useful for averting some crises or managing those that do occur.[43] There are many reasons why learning is difficult (complexity, different interpretations of past, present and future, the rapidity of change, etc.) but it may be especially so in an intense, virtually existential conflict. As noted earlier, it is a crucial issue, if complex and elusive, because many key values that can sustain a peace process – trust, cooperation, empathy – must be learned: they do not always come naturally in the present context.

In the current situation (April 2001) it has become nearly impossible to end the violence and restart the negotiating process because both Arafat and Sharon have locked themselves into a bargaining straitjacket. Sharon says no talks until the violence stops but Arafat seems to think only violence can get him *all* of his goals – i.e., more than Barak offered at Camp David – and thus insists the violence will continue until he gets what he wants (a negotiating process that *begins* where Barak's last offer left off).[44] Either doing what the other wants would thus seem a loss of face and an enormous risk domestically.[45] The only winners are the extremists opposed to any peace agreement: "meaningless" atrocities, as one observer has called them, in fact are very meaningful if they can derail a fragile peace process.

What do these comments suggest about appropriate bargaining strategies? There is a grand debate between two schools of thought – leaving aside the third option of staggering on with a deteriorating status quo until both sides (presumably) come to their senses, an option that is both dangerous and unattractive to all. The first school insists that incremental, brick-by-brick bargaining will not work because of the intensity of the conflict, the total absence of trust, and the pervasive fear that concessions will be interpreted as weakness. Thus only a "big bang" strategy will work. The model here is familiar from Camp David I and II and Dayton: lock the leaders away in some isolated venue, heavy involvement and pressure from a powerful mediator (the United States), the rising political costs of failure for leaders on both sides as expectations rise and their reputations are at stake, and the alluring vision of a reputation as a peacemaker or a candidate for a Nobel Peace Prize. But sometimes the big bang fizzles (as at Camp David II) or continued disagreement on critical issues is obscured or inability or unwillingness to fully implement vague terms is ignored. The high risk/high gain strategy is attractive because it apparently leaps over the usual obstacles by getting the big chiefs into a setting where the costs of failure may seem, at least momentarily, to be greater than the risks of compromise agreement.[46] But if there is no "contract zone" on key substantive issues, if emotions are running too high, and if the enemies of the compromise are strong, not many leaders are going to take the big risks or believe in the big gains.

The alternative seems to be incrementalism, leaving the big issues aside until conditions are more promising and pursuing limited goals that, brick by brick, build bridges to coexistence. Perhaps some limited political agreements will become possible (if initially on peripheral issues) and perhaps even a code of conduct will gradually develop that creates new rules on how to carry on the relationship.[47] But by its very nature an incremental process can be derailed by its slowness in the face of high levels of distrust or by limited gains that do not seem to accumulate or spread to the masses or by the anger generated by terrorist actions or by the lack of clarity about where the process is meant to go. Low risk/low gain may come to seem high risk, no gain.

If these alternatives seem inadequate, what is left? One possibility is to suggest a compromise that might be called "incrementalism plus": an agreement on the minimal long-term goals of both sides (a Palestinian state in nearly all of the West Bank/Gaza and East Jerusalem, and an Israeli commitment to stop all settlement activity in exchange for a strong commitment to stop the violence, stop the illegal purchase of arms, and cease all future demands on Israeli land), with this goal to be pursued in a phased fashion and with strong sanctions for non-compliance. Issues for which no agreement was possible (like the right of return or control of the Temple Mount/*al-Haram al-Sharif*) would require continuous negotiation for a period of time, after which they could be submitted to a mutually-agreed arbitration panel. This kind of agreement would diminish Israeli fears that Arafat would continually raise new demands – the infamous "salami" tactic – and it would provide a period in which (perhaps) enough progress could be made to cool down the "hot" issues and make them amenable to compromise. It would also make clearer what compliance and good behavior would produce and it might generate incentives to comply and not disincentives to cheat. Unfortunately, this argument begs a key question: How do you stop the currently escalating levels of violence so that enough stability can be restored to begin even thinking about bargaining strategies, not win-the-war strategies? (Or the desperate "strategy" of hanging on until the other cracks or something turns up). Given the hard trade-off between guaranteed short-run costs and short-run political risks and the uncertain long-run benefits, this outcome is unsurprising. Still, front-loading benefits, meeting early deadlines, being careful about rhetoric, may at least send some useful signals.

There is another point about bargaining strategies that may be worth mentioning. When the conflict is at its most intense and apparently insoluble state, the only kind of bargaining game that is likely to work is distributional: the narrow exchange of like for like on largely procedural issues. When there is a move toward peace, one hopes to see some form of integrative bargaining emerge in which trade-offs between issues and perhaps resource commitments from external parties permit the size of the pie to be increased. This did not happen either during the initial Oslo negotiations or in the aftermath, perhaps because so little of substance was actually decided by Oslo or perhaps because the United States and other potential donors were not directly involved in the process. In any case, the delays in implementation and the continual accusations of bad faith and non-compliance hardly created an environment conducive to moving beyond distributional bargaining or indeed counterfeit bargaining designed largely to make the other side seem duplicitous.

There is another perspective on the negotiating process in protracted conflicts that may be worth noting, even if its relevance remains to be proved. If the period after a weak peace agreement has some unique characteristics, mixing together persisting conditions of the old conflict and the new conditions or possibilities generated by an initial step toward peace, perhaps we could argue that this period also requires a new approach to bargaining and negotiations, one that builds on but is different from integrative bargaining.[48] This new approach might be described as "transformational bargaining" because the central aim is neither winning the game nor increasing the size of the pie but rather generating new rules and codes of conduct to facilitate long-term peaceful coexistence. This is bound to be an evolutionary process but one that needs to begin affecting behavior in the peace process very quickly – lest we recapitulate the cumulative disasters of the post-Oslo years.[49]

What one needs to try to do in the post-peace agreement period is to deal with the changes that are occurring and the changes that have not yet occurred. Morley argues that negotiations are not about resolving issues or managing a conflict but rather about creating a formula to link what is happening now to what happened in the past and what will happen in the future.[50] Creating an "agreed story" may indeed be helpful over the long term but in the present context it might be considered too abstract or insufficiently aware of the elements of the "conflict ethos" that still persist. It may be more realistic or prudent to suggest that what needs to be done is to shift the bargaining focus from a sole concern with gains for each to a joint concern with individual gains *and* gains for the relationship itself so that each side sees the survival of a viable relationship as a value in itself.[51] This also implies understanding that an important part of the bargaining is subjective and is largely about recognition of identities, status, and legitimacy; once this understanding is achieved, implementation of rules of conduct becomes much easier. This does not imply an effort to deemphasize the importance of gains for each side but rather an attempt to broaden the definition of interests and to weight future gains more heavily.[52]

There have been a number of efforts to suggest rules or codes of conduct for former enemies but most seem to focus on cases where power needs to be shared in a single state between relatively equal partners.[53] Here I am concerned with a related but distinct case: the partitioning of territory between relatively unequal partners. I will merely suggest, tentatively, some possible rules for transformational bargaining. I should emphasize that all these points merely summarize lessons from prior analysis. First and most obviously, there must be an agreement, preferably explicit, to settle all future conflicts of interest peacefully and through a mutually agreed political process. There is usually a willingness to make this pledge when an initial agreement is being negotiated (as with Arafat's commitments at Oslo) but an equal willingness to abandon it when gains seem insufficient or domestic pressures mount. This is a make-or-break issue and perhaps one ought to consider sanctions for non-compliance, especially by mediators, aid agencies, and guarantors. Such sanctions ought to be limited to publicity for early violations but ought to rise in severity with later or more serious violations. Second, borrowing from the theory of consociational democracy, there must be a mutual veto over actions that affect both communities or that have significant cross-border effects. Israel's continual expansion of settlements illustrates the dangers here. Third, despite the mutual recognition implicit in the initial peace agreement, the de facto inequality between the two partners suggests the need for asymmetrical reciprocity: the stronger must be willing to sacrifice some short-run gains for the long-term benefit of the relationship. Fourth, as noted above, while the leader's first task is to ensure that he can increase his own constituency for peace, it is also critical that he understands the needs (and thoughts) of the other leader and is willing to offer support – perhaps hanging together may avert hanging separately. Fifth, leaders must try to avoid forcing confrontations or crises or pushing every dispute to the edge of the abyss – the fabric of the relationship may be too weak to withstand such pressures. Sixth, building peace brick by brick obviously takes time but actions that seem small and insignificant by themselves can accumulate and have significant substantive effects – akin to what happens with the idea in economics of a "cascade of information."[54] Doing things like rewriting biased histories and school texts and changing the rhetoric of confrontation in various arenas can show benign intentions and affect the atmosphere of the relationship. Finally, it helps to build joint institutions that can facilitate cooperation, learning, and mutual awareness. And they may increase the number of people with a felt stake in the peace process.

None of these rules, of course, guarantee a stable peace but implementing them does seem likely to increase the probability that the peace can be strengthened. This is especially true if implementation is accompanied by substantial external financial and political support, providing that support is not wasted in corruption and misconceived expenditures.[55]

Conclusions

Oslo was an exceptionally fragile peace but perhaps the best that could be gotten (or expected) at the time. It gave Arafat and the PLO substantial benefits but it did not provide many benefits to the Palestinian people, it promised negotiations on all the critical issues but it could not and did not guarantee any of the outcomes each side desired, and neither side was able or willing to take the risks implicit in betting on the success of the peace process. As noted, the result was a peace process that became the continuation of conflict by other means. The context of peacemaking was so difficult that failure could easily have been anticipated. Only a different, wiser, and more powerful leadership might have averted the worst.

Given the fact that agreements like Oslo or the Good Friday agreement or the Dayton agreement will always have high risks of failure, why sign them? All of these agreements were top/down agreements and there was very little pressure from below or from the demonstration effect to take the plunge. Still, the elites on both sides, if for very different reasons, could have concluded that even a weak agreement that is badly implemented was a better risk than a status quo that seemed likely to deteriorate. Even if they fail, such agreements may create a floor on which to anchor later negotiations; they break through the immobility, and they may compel some on both sides to begin thinking about what peace is worth and what must be sacrificed to get it. Moreover, some of the risks may be bearable – not all failures to implement are crucial. Agreements are exchanges of conditional promises and there are many reasons to comply with them (including testing the intentions of the other or preserving a reputation for trustworthiness). There are also a variety of means available to decrease vulnerability or to increase the costs of non-compliance.[56] Increasing the incentives to comply may be necessary, especially in the early post-peace period, but if expectations are effectively managed, if some beneficial learning does occur, and if external support is generous, incentives may come to outweigh disincentives.

Nevertheless, gaining sufficient support for the peace process is always going to be a hard sell. Apart from the fact that old attitudes and beliefs will not disappear quickly and that the immediate gains from peace are not likely to be great, there is the intrinsic dilemma of such peaces: there is no way to guarantee that the old enemy is able or willing to implement the peace (let alone deepen it) or that he will not swallow today's concessions and then ask for more. In such circumstances both sides may find it easier to make a case for fighting on because the risks are known and the costs seem bearable and victory – someday – may be possible. And a risky peace process does not have the cognitive legitimacy, especially with the masses, of more, but familiar, conflict.

Thus signing with the full intention of implementing commitments may require a leap of faith.[57] That leap may be justified if the risks of not seeking peace are seen as worse, if some means of reducing the risks (phased implementation, demilitarization, third party guarantees, etc.) are built into the process, and if key leaders recognize (and act on) the belief that the future is not determined – that bad things are possible but not certain. And, presumably some on the other side are likely to see it as in their interest to accept the terms and implement them effectively. In the end, there are no risk-free choices and gambling on a prudent, phased peace process may be as (or more) reasonable than gambling on a crumbling and dangerous status quo.

The gloom and doom surrounding current circumstances is surely justified. At a minimum, an opportunity has been lost; at a maximum, both sides might slide even deeper into violence and hatred and perhaps even generate a regional war. Nevertheless, it is very important to emphasize another aspect of the Oslo process. A few years ago a US official was asked to assess the progress in Bosnia since the signing of the Dayton agreement. He replied:

> If you judge by Dayton [that is, the terms of the agreement] there is noncompliance everywhere you look . . . But if you judge by the standard of a peace process [over twenty or thirty years], this thing is going at warp speed.[58]

There is a useful lesson implicit in this comment. The terms of Oslo have obviously not been met but Oslo also has a deeper layer of meaning. If one looks beyond the violence, one could argue that Oslo broke the mold and forced each side for the first time to confront questions obscured by the conflict itself: how much is peace really worth and how much can we or must we give up for an opportunity to live in peace? Confronted with these questions both sides – leaders and followers alike – have retreated into the comfortable pieties of the past and into mutual accusations of deceit and bad faith. When and if the peace process is revived, it may well be that both sides will have learned useful lessons about how to run and not run a peace process. In effect, even if Oslo is in ruins, it will have left traces in the sand that future peacemakers will not be able to ignore or forget.

There are a few simple and obvious precepts that might make future negotiations more likely to succeed. Simple and obvious they may be but they are too often forgotten or ignored in the context of intense conflict. Most of these precepts refer to attitudes that both sides need to bring to the negotiations or priorities that they need to set. In a sense, they seek to broaden the cognitive legitimacy of the peace process to both sides, elites and public alike.

(1) Borrowing from a literary expression – synecdoche – do not mistake the actions of a part for the actions of the whole. We all "know" on some intellectual level that not all Palestinians are terrorists and not all Israelis are Baruch Goldsteins. But we also speak loosely when we say "the Palestinians" or "the Israelis" do not "really" want peace, when in fact some do, others don't, and yet others shift attitudes quickly in response to what the *other* does do. We forget all these distinctions too easily in the context of the latest atrocity, especially when media and texts depict the other as evil and corrupt. It pays to remember that peace will always be opposed by some and that the peace does not require unanimity in either camp but rather enough on both sides to form a viable (and, one hopes, growing) coalition for peace. In any case, neither will be able to see potential partners for peace if neither can differentiate between potential allies and real enemies.[59]

(2) A second precept borrows from the first rule of medicine: do no harm. Joining a peace process merely to gain leverage in the conflict or with no intention of full implementation or with the intention of using violence as a means to force concessions can only succeed in destroying the peace.

It is a useless counsel of perfection to insist that none of these should be done, given the inevitable doubts that a fragile peace can survive. Still, if the leaders at least are genuinely committed to the peace process, destabilizing and destructive actions may be limited, contained, and unnecessary. As noted above, failure here means that the leader will lose credibility with the other side and lose also the ability to make the necessary conditional promises that are the basis of any agreement. Failure also means later agreements will be progressively harder to negotiate.

(3) Everyone agrees that the peace process requires strong leaders that are willing to talk truthfully to their followers, that have the courage to do more than hide behind their extremists, that understand that the post-peace period will require new patterns of thought and action, and that have the courage to make clear that there is no such thing as a cheap peace, a peace without painful compromises. The conflict between Israel and the Palestinians has had only caricatures of this ideal, although Rabin might well have risen to the occasion had he lived. The problem is that the evolution of the conflict tends to generate weak leaders limited by ambivalent domestic support and rising opposition to compromise. Perhaps only a mediator who provides strong cover for necessary compromises and strong promises of aid can help this situation. The other apparent option, increasingly discussed in recent months, is to await the arrival of a new generation of leaders, which could be a costly wait – and there is no guarantee that they would be much better. One needs also to be aware that talk of the need for a new leader may only further weaken support for the existing leader, thus making the negotiating process even more unstable. Perhaps trying to strengthen the old leader may be a more prudent course than waiting for salvation by the arrival of a new savior.

(4) There is widespread agreement among analysts of the negotiating process that any agreement will be unstable unless it is perceived as fair and equitable by both sides. The problem with this, of course, is that there is usually complete disagreement between the parties about what equity or fairness means. The problem is compounded by the lack of empathy, which implies that each dismisses the other's claims as spurious or irrelevant.[60] Here asymmetrical reciprocity by the stronger side could be helpful in smoothing over subjective conflicts, as could an emphasis on apologies for past sins.[61] Perhaps also this could be joined to a sense of asymmetrical equity: the grievances and resentments of the rebel side may be deeper and thus unilateral gestures by the stronger may have a disproportionately beneficial impact. In the short run, given the complexity of this issue, perhaps it would be better to try to avoid focusing on fairness and equity, and instead concentrate on practical compromises that can produce quick benefits for the public at large.

(5) One problem has been intrinsic to the kind of peace process described

above. This is that all the short-run calculations of interests and actions work out the wrong way. It is rational to make only tentative commitments, to delay implementation, and to cheat where the likelihood of being caught and the penalties for being caught are small, if you distrust the other side and if you doubt his willingness or ability to offer a compromise more attractive than the status quo. In these circumstances any agreement is likely to unravel before it can produce enough benefits to begin to seem valuable. In effect, to borrow a term that is currently fashionable at the World Bank with regard to structural adjustment programs, no one seems to "own" the peace agreement in the sense of feeling it is a valuable possession that should be protected and nurtured.

This brings us to the final precept, one that is endlessly relevant for problems of cooperation in an anarchic world: take the long-run seriously or as the economists say, lower the discount rate on the future. If both sides remain entirely focused on short-run, zero-sum games or games of chicken or blind man's bluff, the prognosis is for more of the same (if we are lucky) or a steadily deteriorating blood bath with potentially disastrous regional consequences. Decisions that seem too painful or even dangerous to make now might be calculated differently if each side thought more about what the relationship might look like in ten years if such decisions are not taken now and such risks run now before they become much worse in the years ahead. This little exercise in mental gymnastics is unlikely to affect the calculations of the extremists who believe that both God and time are on their side but whether it can somehow intrude on the calculations of weak leaders intent, above all, on retaining power is unclear. Unless it does, however, whether from the emergence of new leaders, or severe pressures from key patrons, or from a terrible "shock" that finally generates enough pressure so that most come to believe "enough is enough," the race to the bottom may not be over.

Notes

1   Complaints about the corruption, brutality and incompetency of Mr. Arafat's regime have been widespread even within the Palestinian community. For example, see the severe criticisms in a joint statement by twenty Palestinian notables reported in *The New York Times*, November 29, 1999, p. A7. Mr. Arafat provided abundant evidence of the accuracy of the indictment by promptly jailing seven of the signers, shooting another, and threatening the rest.

2   Edward Said has long advocated the creation of a binational state in which Israelis and Palestinians share power and live together peacefully. See Edward W. Said, *The End of the Peace Process – Oslo and After* (New York: Pantheon Books, 2000). Since this would involve the destruction of the idea of a Jewish state and since it would give the Palestinians only shared sovereignty, this is a

peace proposal with a unique characteristic: it is completely rejected by both sides. Apart from the obvious fact that the escalation of violence and radical rhetoric has made living together peacefully seem ever more utopian, the pursuit of this "solution" and the dismissal of the Oslo process and whatever succeeds it loses the opportunity to make moderate gains that can be built on and generates more support for extremist options that could destroy any hope of progress toward peace.

3   For criticism of Arafat by the former US Negotiator Dennis Ross, see Clyde Haberman, "Dennis Ross's Exit Interview," *The New York Times Magazine*, March 27, 2001, pp. 38–9. For a bizarre assault on former President Clinton, who pushed the Israeli government to make the Palestinians the most generous offer they have ever received, see the excerpts from a memorandum issued by the Palestinian Media Center under the auspices of the Palestinian Authority in *The New York Times*, January 23, 2001, p. A10.

4   The violence is embittering and polarizing but it does not always impinge heavily on daily life and adaptations have been made to the other costs. As one analyst said of Northern Ireland, "the current situation is unsatisfactory to all the contending parties, but it is not the worst conceivable. [The parties] hold on to what advantages they have, lest in the course of bargaining they lose even more than they already have." John Whyte, "Dynamics of Social and Political Change in Northern Ireland," in Dermot Keogh and Michael H. Haltzel, eds., *Northern Ireland and the Politics of Reconciliation* (Cambridge: Cambridge University Press, 1993), p. 116. One ought not leave the impression here that the domestication of protracted conflict – learning to live with its traumas – is cost free: *inter alia*, there is a coarsening of civic virtue, a devaluation of democratic norms, and a destruction of empathy.

5   A number of rebel groups, after discovering victory is not imminent, have adopted a "long war" strategy to minimize short-run losses and keep the "dream" alive. See for example Brendan O'Brien, *The Long War: The IRA and Sin Fein, 1985 to Today* (Syracuse: Syracuse University Press, 1995).

6   For a more detailed treatment of these conditions see my essay "In Fear of Peace: Getting Past Maybe," in Robert L. Rothstein, ed., *After the Peace: Resistance and Reconciliation* (Boulder, CO: Lynne Rienner Publishers, 1999), pp. 1–25. On the "conflictive ethos" and the way in which it enables a society to adapt to conflict, see the interesting piece by Daniel Bar-Tal, "From Intractable Conflict Through Conflict Resolution to Reconciliation: Psychological Analysis," *Political Psychology*, Vol. 21, No. 2 (2000), pp. 351–65.

7   See Meron Benvenisti, *Intimate Enemies – Jews and Arabs in a Shared Land* (Berkeley, CA: University of California Press, 1995), pp. 77–88 and 199–200, for an argument about the existential nature of the Israeli–Palestinian Conflict.

8   The absence of empathy is also part of the reason why the response of one side to an atrocity committed against the other is rarely an expression of genuine sympathy but rather a restatement of what has been done to us by them in the past – if not an actual expression of joy at the suffering of the other, as if it allayed my own pain.

9   The dilemma is that a gradual, incremental peace process is likely to fail because of the use of violence by the extremists, the slowness in achieving significant material benefits from peace, and the inability of weakened leaders to manage rising expectations effectively. Conversely, the conditions necessary for successful "big bang" negotiations are rarely present. Thus neither a low risk/low gain nor a high risk/high gain strategy seems likely to work, a point to which we shall return.

10   Richard Rose quoted in John McGarry and Brendan O'Leary, *Explaining Northern Ireland – Broken Images* (Oxford: Blackwell Publishers, 1995), p. 354. Note that Rose seemed largely correct for about two decades but that gradual changes were occurring – politically, psychologically, economically – that finally led, as with Oslo, to a tentative breakthrough in the mid-1990s.

11   While the existential elements of the conflict seemed to abate immediately after the Oslo Accord was signed, the resumption of terrorism, armed attacks, and riots has regenerated feelings about an existential threat – particularly in Israel where the feeling that "we are back to 1948" has grown even among some of the people who were once among Oslo's strongest supporters.

12   Much of the literature on internal conflicts, borrowing a term made popular by I. W. Zartman, uses the term "ripe moment" where I have used the term "window of opportunity." I prefer the latter for a number of reasons that I will discuss in a forthcoming piece but note here only that Zartman's term is something of a tautology, that the notion of a specific "moment" is misleading and not well specified, and that it misses the complexity of the different strands that must come together to get a tentative break-through toward peace. Zartman also argues that the ripe moment will come when there is a "mutually hurting stalemate" but this too is not well specified: the mutually hurting stalemate can go on for a long time before a ripe moment suddenly appears. See I. William Zartman, "Dynamics and Constraints in Negotiations in Internal Conflicts," in Zartman, ed., *Elusive Peace: Negotiating an End to Civil Wars* (Washington, DC: The Brookings Institution, 1995), pp. 3–29.

13   Trade-offs in the initial stage will be discussed below.

14   I shall discuss later how such efforts might be generated and strengthened.

15   Demands for full and complete implementation of all Palestinian commitments at Oslo (especially on terrorism) might seem reasonable in this context but asking for too much too quickly, as Prime Minister Netanyahu did with Chairman Arafat, may thus be a disguised way to undermine the agreement or to weaken the enemy leader. For an interesting discussion of this argument, see Ian S. Lustick, "Ending Protracted Conflicts: The Oslo Peace Process Between Political Partnership and Legality," *Cornell International Law Journal*, Vol. 30, No 3 (1997), pp. 741–57.

16   In this regard Arafat failed miserably as his rhetoric in private ("the struggle continues," etc.) differed from his rhetoric in public (constant assertions about the need for a "peace of the brave," which rapidly became a joke on both sides), which greatly increased suspicion and doubt about Oslo. His creation of a corrupt, brutal, and incompetent PA did not help matters. On this, see Glen E. Robinson, "The Growing Authoritarianism of the Arafat Regime," *Survival*, Vol. 39, No. 2 (Summer 1997), pp. 42–56. Robinson says that the fact

that Arafat has become a despot is surprising but I do not find it surprising given his background, his experiences as a frequently challenged rebel leader, the weakening of his position (especially after support for Saddam Hussein's invasion and brutalization of Kuwait), and the lack of strong popular support for Oslo.

17 Conviction about the other's lack of seriousness and the fear of being duped are, as noted earlier, intrinsic to these kinds of peace processes. The lack of trust thus generates negative self-fulfilling processes, which implies that both sides (and external supporters) must be aware of this and understand the need to take actions that generate increases in trust. Since building trust is obviously time-consuming and since cooperative policies must be implemented from the beginning of the peace process many analysts argue that overlapping interests must be and can be a sufficient basis for cooperation. I am doubtful, however, that in the fraught context of protracted conflict a sense of shared interests will suffice (or perhaps even be perceived). This suggests that, since trust and coop-eration are largely learned patterns of behavior, a successful peace process will require leaders who seek to generate a learning process that sends the proper signals or lessons to the other side – which did not happen after Oslo. On learning trust, see Kenneth Clark and Martin Sefton, "The Sequential Prisoner's Dilemma: Evidence on Reciprocation," *The Economic Journal*, Vol. 111 (January 2001), pp. 51–68.

18 If leaders on both sides understood this context more clearly, they might also understand a crucial piece of tactical advice: don't push to the edge of the abyss because there may not be any exit strategy. This seems to be the situation that Arafat and Sharon have now blundered into: extreme statements about what the other must do or commit to before talks can begin again. On how stronger and wiser leaders in South Africa avoided going over the abyss – although they got close to it at times – see Pierre du Toit, "South Africa In Search of Post-Settlement Peace," in John Darby and Roger MacGinty, eds., *The Management of Peace Processes* (London: Macmillan, 2000), pp. 30–1.

19 Lustick has argued for a high-risk, high-gain strategy in the Oslo process but my argument attempts to explain why it is very likely that a low-risk, low-gain strategy will be chosen and, indeed, why the high-risk strategy, were it to be chosen by both sides, might end very badly – as happened with Arafat, Barak, and Clinton at Camp David II. For the counter argument, see Ian S. Lustick "Necessary Risks: Lessons for the Israeli-Palestinian Peace Process from Ireland and Algeria," *Middle East Policy*, Vol. 3, No. 3 (1994), p. 42ff.

20 The quote is from Eamonn Mallie and David McKitrick, *The Fight for Peace – The Secret Story Behind the Irish Peace Process* (London: Heinemann, 1996), p. 349. I shall speak further below about the contrast between what strong and weak leaders can risk.

21 Yossi Beilin notes that Abu Mazen, a very high-ranking Palestinian official, told him (Beilin) at Oslo that the Palestinian leadership before Oslo took pride in knowing nothing about Israel and the Israelis: why bother if Israel was to be destroyed? So Israel was demonized and no distinction was made between different views or perspectives. See Yossi Beilin, *Touching Peace – From the Oslo Accord to a Final Agreement* (London: Weidenfeld and Nicolson, 1999),

p. 168. Perhaps this commitment to ignorance about the enemy helps to explain why Arafat took so many actions that undermined the Israeli peace movement. In any case, ignorance and demonization do not encourage empathy.

22 There will be more discussion of this level with the fourth point below.

23 For two-level bargaining games, see Peter B. Evans, Harold K. Jacobsen, and Robert D. Putnam, eds., *Double-edged Diplomacy: International Bargaining and Domestic Politics* (Berkeley: University of California Press, 1993). Note that even the notion of a three-level game may sometimes oversimplify, as in Northern Ireland where one could specify a direct Loyalists–Nationalist level, a Belfast–London level, a Belfast–Dublin level, and a London–Dublin level – not to mention the domestic levels for all the parties to the conflict.

24 For one interesting example of the current focus on the importance, if not the dominance, of domestic politics, see Helen V. Milner, *Interests, Institutions and Information: Domestic Politics and International Relations* (Princeton: Princeton University Press, 1997).

25 For testimony in this regard about Arafat, see Haberman, "Dennis Ross's Exit Interview" and Mohamed Rabiel, *US–PLO Dialogue – Secret Diplomacy and Conflict Resolution* (Gainesville, FL: University of Florida Press, 1995, pp. 46–56. It is unclear whether rebel leaders, always insecure and threatened, exhibit these tendencies in a more flagrant form than government leaders – as the economists say, it all depends.

26 Most peace processes in protracted conflicts are top/down in form, which also generates the common problem of how to develop grassroots support. One apparent exception is the Basque conflict, where pressures for peace were driven by both popular demands and the "demonstration effect" of the Good Friday agreement in Northern Ireland. See Ludger Mees, "The Basque Peace Process, Nationalism and Political Violence," in Darby and MacGinty, *The Management of Peace Processes*, pp. 172–4 and 175–6.

27 We shall return to these issues below.

28 See Tamar Hermann and David Newman, "A Path Strewn with Thorns: Along the Difficult Road of Israeli–Palestinian Peacemaking," in Darby and MacGinty, *The Management of Peace Processes*, pp. 43–5.

29 Even prominent peaceniks like the novelist Amos Oz began to express serious doubts about whether Arafat was ever serious about peace or – worse yet – whether peace with the Palestinians would ever be possible. More and more people began to refer to the years of struggle after 1948 as if the past had been resurrected in an even more malignant form.

30 The political philosopher Hannah Arendt was one of the first to point out the importance of being able to make credible promises in politics. It is especially important in the present context where doubts about the other's true intentions are inevitable. For a brief discussion of Arendt's views, see Ronald A. Wells, *People Behind the Peace: Community and Reconciliation in Northern Ireland* (Grand Rapids, MI: Wm. B. Erdmans, 1999), pp. 40–1.

31 The leader's primary initial task is obviously to rally domestic support for peace, without which he will quickly fall – or quickly have to abandon the peace process. But it takes two leaders and two constituencies for peace to

stabilize and deepen. Thus, each leader is also a key figure in helping (or hurting) the other's efforts to build support. The leader's task is dual because he has so much at stake in how well the other performs, something which neither Arafat nor Netanyahu seemed to understand or care about. In addition, neither Arafat nor Netanyahu made even minimal efforts to educate their own people about the compromises necessary for peace, whether from weakness or lack of conviction about peace is unclear. Or perhaps it was simply too dangerous in terms of each's domestic constituency, which offered support based on an image of militancy.

32 The dilemmas faced by weak leadership also raises questions about the commonsensical notion that the longer a peace process goes on, the more the leader has invested in it and the more he needs some face-saving compromise. But the situation is more complex than this because it depends on the alternatives available, the nature of the gains in the compromise, the extent of internal and external pressures to reach agreement, and subjective judgments about whether time is or is not on one's side.

33 See du Toit, "South Africa: In Search of Post-Settlement Peace," p. 29.

34 For an excellent review of the weaknesses of Palestinian institutions, see *Strengthening Palestinian Public Institutions* (Report of an Independent Task Force sponsored by the Council on Foreign Relations, with Yezid Sayegh and Khalil Shikaki as Principal Authors, New York, 1999) and Glen E. Robinson, *Building a Palestinian State: The Incomplete Revolution* (Bloomington, IN: Indiana University Press, 1997).

35 Haberman, "Dennis Ross's Exit Interview," p. 38.

36 Hermann and Newman, "A Path Strewn with Thorns," pp. 119–20.

37 When Arafat publicly raised demands for a "right of return" for several million Palestinian refugees to Israel itself and for complete sovereignty over the Temple Mount/*Haram al-Sharif*, which was obviously also a revered religious site for Jews, he was not only falling in behind his own extremists but also signaling the Israelis that he had lost interest in peace and wanted only victory. One is reminded here of a statement by Heinlein, the leader of the Czech Germans, in 1938: "We must always demand so much that we cannot be satisfied." Quoted in Arthur Aughey, "A New Beginning? The Prospects for a Politics of Civility in Northern Ireland," in Joseph Ruane and Jennifer Todd, eds., *After the Good Friday Agreement* (Dublin: University College Dublin Press, 1999), p. 140.

38 Note that the divergent responses to weakness – one seeking to use more violence to get more gains, the other offering more concessions in hopes of overcoming domestic dissent by reaching a comprehensive settlement – suggests the difficulties of deriving simple propositions about the varied effects of domestic politics on peace processes.

39 To return to an earlier metaphor, the painters/peacemakers in Northern Ireland drew a few more lines (about power sharing, peaceful resolution of disputes, a principle of majority consent), but left the big issue of Northern Ireland's political fate unsettled. Oslo was a more problematic agreement because its initial benefits were largely procedural, it settled nothing of substance, and it provided no picture of a final agreement or of a principle to

guide the decision-making process. In part, this reflects the difference between a case where power-sharing in one entity is an obvious choice and the more difficult and complex issues involved in dividing a territory both consider their own.

40 For discussions of the requirements of this stage, see my "Fragile Peace and Its Aftermath," in Rothstein, *After the Peace*, pp. 223–47 and Bar-Tal, "From Intractable Conflict Through Conflict Resolution to Reconciliation."

41 This is one of the benefits of the many "second track" negotiations that may occasionally benefit the peace process itself but are probably more important in keeping lines of communication open even in the worst of times and in exploring options that are difficult to deal with in formal talks because of fears of losing face or appearing weak.

42 Some Palestinians are even beginning to question the use of violence as a bargaining tactic, "gingerly asking if their leaders have a strategy that justifies the devastating loss of life, property, mobility and income." Deborah Sontag, "Palestinians Delicately Begin Debate on Circle of Violence," *The New York Times*, March 9, 2001, p. A1 and p. A8. There are obviously risks in doing so because even the appearance of disloyalty has been punished severely – including assassination.

43 See George W. Breslauer, "What Have We Learned About Learning?" in George W. Breslauer and Philip E. Tetlock, eds., *Learning in US and Soviet Foreign Policy* (Boulder, CO: Westview Press, 1991), pp. 830–51. Since it seems clear that deeper assumptions about the enemy and about appropriate behavior are unlikely to change until the peace process is widely perceived as stable and beneficial – which may take more than a decade – the crucial immediate question is whether and how the peace process can survive when old ideas still prevail and new ideas are largely about tactical adjustments. Perhaps adapted behavior-choosing new means but not new ends-will suffice until the peace process begins to show its worth.

44 The latter demand, of course, violates standard bargaining rules (nothing is decided until everything is decided, which implies partial concessions in a failed negotiation do not bind later negotiators), rules that the Palestinians themselves insisted on (according to an Israeli negotiator). Arafat's use of violence brings to mind an old Arab proverb: When the only tool you have is a hammer, every problem looks like a nail.

45 The fact that both sides have backed themselves into a rhetorical corner is rather like the current crisis over decommissioning of arms in Northern Ireland. Either the relinquishing of arms by the IRA or acceptance of the fact that they will not relinquish them by the Protestant community will be seen as a defeat: thus stalemate and a growing threat to the peace itself. Making one demand too far can turn a practical issue, about which some compromises are possible, into a symbolic issue that cannot be compromised.

46 I pointed out earlier that it is not always true that leaders will finally compromise because their reputations will suffer if a prolonged and highly publicized negotiation fails. Much depends on the available alternatives, propensity for risk, and other factors.

47 For suggestions in this regard by Dennis Ross, see Jane Perlez, "U.S. Mideast

Envoy Recalls the Day Pandora's Box Wouldn't Shut," *The New York Times*, January 29, 2001, p. A4.

48 The period after a weak peace agreement has been signed thus has some unique characteristics-which also bear some resemblance to the period after a new democracy has been established on rather shaky grounds. For more detailed comment, see my "Fragile Peace and Its Aftermath."

49 I should hasten to add that the comments that follow are very tentative and incomplete. They are provided here only indicatively.

50 One example of Morley's argument is in Ian E. Morley, "Intra-organizational Bargaining," in Jean F. Hartley and Geoffrey M. Stevenson, eds., *Employment Relations: The Psychology of Influence and Control at Work* (Oxford: Blackwell, 1992), pp. 203–24.

51 This is akin to the notion that the states in the nineteenth-century balance of power system sought individual gains but not to the point that such gains would threaten the system itself. A sense of restraint, of playing by mutually agreed rules, of trying not to push potential allies to the edge kept conflicts – most conflicts – from getting out of hand. It helped, of course, to have a common enemy in mind: revolutionary threats to political stability.

52 Where power is asymmetrically divided it might also imply the need for asymmetrical equity (a willingness by the stronger to accept lesser gains in the short run).

53 There is an interesting discussion of the need for a "politics of civility" in Northern Ireland in Arthur Aughey, "A New Beginning? The Prospects for a Politics of Civility in Northern Ireland," in Ruane and Todd, *After the Good Friday Agreement*, pp. 122–44.

54 This fits with the notion that small actions can, over time, produce larger than anticipated effects.

55 Arafat insisted that a substantial portion of the aid he received be invested in the creation and arming of eight security forces (over 40,000 individuals). According to Israeli sources, he spent even more on secret and illegal imports of other weapons. This has increased the ability of the Palestinians to engage in armed conduct or to undertake terrorist actions. But the opportunity costs have been great: money diverted from more productive efforts to accelerate development, an escalation of the level of violent exchanges with the Israelis, and the conviction in Israel that Israeli citizens would not get security from peace-and that Arafat had proved that he could not be trusted.

56 For a useful discussion of this issue, see Richard B. Bilder, *Managing the Risks of International Agreement* (Madison, WI: University of Wisconsin Press, 1981).

57 Suspicion that the rebel side is only accepting today's offer as a stage before asking for more later is widespread: a compromise agreement reflects momentary inability to achieve all goals but not a relinquishing of those goals. As fears grew in Israel that the use of violence and the hatred pouring out of the "street" (and Arafat's media) meant that the Palestinians would never accept Israel's right to exist in peace, questions also began to grow about giving up anything new if it was to be used only as a platform for more demands. Similar fears arose in Northern Ireland about the IRA's view that the Good Friday agree-

ment was only a stage on the way to Irish unification. See Jennifer Todd, "Nationalism, Republicanism and the Good Friday Agreement" in Ruane and Todd, *After the Good Friday Agreement*, p. 57 ff.

58   Quoted in R. Jeffrey Smith, "U.S. Sees Long Foreign Role in Bosnia," *The International Herald Tribune*, December 29, 1997, p. 5.

59   I already have noted that I am doubtful about the workability of the common-sense notion that all who have the power to overturn the peace process ought to be brought into it. The cost may be too high if they demand too much or if they intend to act as "spoilers." In such cases, they need to be isolated and fought.

60   The problem is especially severe with apparently indivisible and symbolic issues like the Temple Mount/*Haram al-Sharif*. The sensible advice to turn such issues into pragmatic, divisible issues is not easy to follow. The complex issue of what constitutes a just or fair settlement deserves more detailed comment than I can give it here. For a useful analysis, see David A. Welch, *Justice and the Genesis of War* (Cambridge: Cambridge University Press, 1993).

61   There is an interesting discussion of this issue in Donald W. Shriver, Jr., "The Long Road to Reconciliation: Some Moral Stepping-Stones," in Rothstein, *After the Peace*, pp. 207–22.

The Pursuit of Israeli–Palestinian Peace: A Retrospective

Aaron Miller

The purpose of this chapter is to look honestly, openly, and critically at the Oslo Process – what it achieved, what it didn't achieve, what about it is worth preserving and what must go by the wayside. It is essential that before we know where we are going, we try to understand where we have been.

First and foremost, I believe it is inappropriate and irrelevant to talk about whether or not Oslo as a process is alive or dead. It is too late for that. The legacy of Oslo, for good or for ill, has shaped the pursuit of Israeli–Palestinian peace in a way that will be very hard to reverse. The legacy of Oslo will likely provide the foundation and to some degree a measure of direction for the future. There are *six aspects* of this legacy that deserve to be discussed. The *first* is the issue of mutual recognition, when in September 1993, Israel and the embodiment of Palestinian nationalism, the organizational embodiment of Palestinian nationalism, the PLO, recognized one another's mutual right to exist. They converted an existential conflict over physical and political identity into a political conflict over borders, over refugees, over security, over Jerusalem, that could be resolved. The issue of mutual recognition is almost irreversible. When you recognize an adversary it is very hard to unrecognize, to take back what you have given, and in recognizing the fact that they were partners Israel and the Palestinians in their own way transcended and undermined a generation of mythologies and ideology. The partnership is definitely uneasy at this point, and indeed it could be described as adversarial, but it is impossible to deny the issue of mutual recognition.

Second, permanent status negotiations, deferred according to an Oslo timetable but ultimately joined, were one of Oslo's most fundamental and radical departures. An Israel and Palestinian commitment for the first time in their history to put issues that were heretofore unthinkable on the negotiating table was very hard to do for each side. For Israelis to put an issue like Jerusalem on the table, for Palestinians who believe in implementation more than in the negotiation process, to discuss territory was very hard. Once an issue is on the table, neither side is going to get everything they want. My perception is that as a result of Oslo, it is impossible to reverse this process now.

Third, Oslo reflected a fundamentally imperfect relationship between two people who were trying desperately to find a way out of a historic struggle. But it changed the situation on the ground, if very imperfectly. Current realities reflect broken commitments and promises, mutual anger and mutual resentment. But two basic facts and processes were created. (1) Israel, to use the words of Oslo, redeployed from the West Bank and withdrew from Gaza, and (2) the Palestinians began to create institutions, however imperfect they may be, of their national life. The realities on the ground are now fundamentally difficult if not impossible to alter.

And *fourth*, what was Oslo a response to in the end? It was a response to one basic reality: that the Israeli–Palestinian problem has no status quo. It will not stay the way it is because Israelis and Palestinians – unlike Israelis and Syrians, unlike Israelis and Jordanians, unlike Israelis and Egyptians, and unlike Israelis and Lebanese – are both products of proximity. Proximity is what mandates no status quo. And if there is no status quo in a problem, there has to be change. Change can be bad and violent, tragic and sad. But change can also produce opportunities for accommodation. Oslo was more about starting than it was about continuing or ending. And this in essence was its logic. Oslo was built on the logic of transition. How else do you overcome the complicated situation that Israelis and Palestinians found themselves in? It is all very well to talk about incrementalism or transition. But first you have to talk about how to start a peace process. Later transition brought with it uncertainty and ambiguity; with the result of no clear objective or goal. As a consequence, inevitably, Oslo was flawed because it offered Palestinians and Israelis a departure point but it could not promise or guarantee, either in the negotiations, the agreements themselves, or the implementation of those agreements, where they would ultimately go.

Oslo also had to contend with one fundamental fact that neither Israelis nor Palestinians could change, namely an asymmetry of power. In most negotiations, an asymmetry of power has to somehow be converted into a balance of interests. But this was impossible under the Oslo circumstances. Even prior to Oslo, this issue was particularly difficult for Palestinians. I recall that in the eight or nine negotiating sessions that were held in Washington after the Madrid Conference in October 1991, how difficult it was to watch Israelis and Palestinians deal with each other, but how uplifting it was also to watch Israelis and Palestinians come to Washington and negotiate around a table as equals, with respect and a measure of dignity that was hitherto lacking. It was distressing to observe that once the negotiations adjourned, Israelis and Palestinians returned to an active lower level but ongoing conflict. I do not wish to moralize or to assign blame, but the *reality of an asymmetry of power, which could not be converted into a balance of interests*, made it extremely difficult for both sides.

Settlement activity was a major problem from the Palestinian perspective. In 1992 there were 100,000 Israelis living beyond the Green Line, in 2000 there were 200,000; that is a doubling of the population during the period of the negotiations from 1993 to 2000. Settlements, territory, and borders were issues that were to be addressed in permanent status negotiations. They were not to be prejudiced and predetermined before those permanent status negotiations began. This was one feature of an asymmetrical situation which bred frustration and mistrust, and I believe severely handicapped the Oslo process.

If asymmetry of power was a problem from the Palestinian point of view, then Palestinian behavior during the course of the Oslo process was a huge problem for the Israelis, particularly on the security side. And here there was another asymmetry. If, in fact, renunciation of violence and terrorism was the entry card – the entry point, reflected in the exchange of letters between Rabin and Arafat in September 1993 – then from the Israeli perspective there was little sense of delivery. Albeit that there was security cooperation, and at times there was a unilateral effort on the part of the Palestinian Authority to deal with the activities of Hamas and Islamic Jihad. But from the Israeli perspective, while 100 percent results were not expected, 100 percent effort was expected. And that is not what the Israelis believed was happening. It was episodic at best. And as a consequence of that fact, even though between 1998 and 2000 Israeli experienced the fewest number of terrorist attacks and fatalities in Israel's history, Israeli fatalities doubled during the period 1988 to 1993, and doubled again from 1993 to 1997. This was a major problem because it cut at the core of what the Israelis believed they expected form the Oslo process.

Another issue was the socialization of hostility and grievance, as reflected in Palestinian media treatment. If the Palestinians couldn't abide by Israeli settlement activity, because it prejudged and predetermined issues reserved for negotiations, Israelis increasingly asked themselves the question, Why are our partners continuing to socialize hostility and grievance? And even though most Israelis were prepared to accept the fact that there was resentment and anger as a consequence of Palestinian dependency, this could not excuse the Palestinian Authority's seeming acquiescence or support for this kind of media education. Hence the asymmetry of power and the asymmetry of behavior when it came to security and issues like socialization of grievance made it extremely difficult to create trust and confidence. The logic of Oslo was to defer for now issues that could not be resolved on the assumption that over time confidence and trust would be deposited in the bank. This pool of currency would grow so that even while Jerusalem could not be resolved in 1993, a solution could be worked out later. This was a huge problem because from the perspective of the respective Israeli publics and Palestinian publics a huge gap existed between the world of negotiatiors and the populations on whose behalf they were acting on.

Fifth, the Oslo process created for the first time in the history of the Israeli–Palestinian conflict a process between the Israelis and Palestinians in which they were both heavily invested. There is no question about it. However imperfect the process, four Israeli prime ministers accepted grudgingly, perhaps unwillingly, certain aspects of the Oslo Accords. And the PLO and the Palestinian Authority invested in this process even when their critics and opposition told them that they shouldn't. The process created sufficient basis for cooperation for both parties to enter into permanent status negotiations. But it wasn't enough. There wasn't enough trust and confidence to allow Palestinians and Israelis, when it came time as it did in the spring and summer of 2000, to begin addressing and dealing with the core issues. The Oslo process did not provide the trust and confidence that was required. There was the gap between the world of the negotiatiors and the world on the ground. Then there were two fundamental different points of departure, which psychologically made permanent status negotiations very difficult. The points of departure are not intractable, but they are extremely difficult. The Palestinian departure point, at least among those that accept the notion that a Palestinian state should be created alongside of, instead of in place of Israel, was that a Palestinian state would be the outcome of the peace process. This Palestinian viewpoint is that 78 percent of historic Palestine is gone, 22 percent is left. "It is ours by right, it is ours through a sense of entitlement, it's our." Therefore any fundamental compromise from the 22 percent is a major problem for Palestinians. The Israelis start from a different point of departure. "Yes, we are willing to engage in a political process, yes we are willing to negotiate a permanent status agreement with you, and yes we understand your logic, but you have to accept the fact that our security and demographic needs and requirements will have to come out of your peace." Those two departure points ensured, with or without a successful Oslo process, that the logic of permanent status talks would be very difficult. The issues that Israelis and Palestinians were negotiating were fundamentally different than the issues that Arabs and Israelis had negotiated, either in the first Camp David, the Israelis–Jordanian Peace Treaty of 1984, or the episodic but very serious efforts between the Israelis and the Syrians to negotiate which concluded in March 2000. That is because, of the four core issues that constitute the Israeli–Palestinian permanent status issues, security and territory are negotiable and tractable, but the issues of refugees and Jerusalem are virtually intractable because they involve issues of identity. They are in essence identity issues that don't lend themselves to maps and security arrangements. They cut to the core of the conflict and the sense of history and religion and historical consciousness of both peoples. And as a consequence the burden on the permanent status negotiations of these two issues is tremendous.

Sixth, if you had a process that achieved much but didn't achieve all, was there an alternative? It may be a historical question but it is still a fundamentally important question because it gets to the issue of whether the perfect is in fact the enemy of the good in a conflict where there is no perfect justice. This concept seems to me quite compelling, for there will not be perfect justice from both sides, only imperfect solutions in an imperfect world. Policy is often a choice between imperfect alternatives: pick one, it's better than the other; or don't pick any and sit there and just wait. In my judgment the issue was not whether or not there was another alternative to Oslo, there was no other alternative than to start.

Nevertheless, it is pertinent to ask whether Olso could have been improved. Could confidence and trust been increased, the process of implementation improved, a better relationship between Israelis and Palestinians established, a variety of people to people programs created to address the issues of images and stereotypes? The chapters that follow will address some of these issues.

So where does Oslo fit in the grand scheme of things? I would argue, and have argued, that over the last fifteen years there have been three departure points in the Arab–Israeli conflict, subsequent to the first Camp David, which have created a critical mass of formal and informal agreements. This makes it very difficult for Israelis and Palestinians, or Arabs and Israeli, to go back. An Arab–Israeli peace is not inevitable, but what has been achieved is not easily reversed. The first departure point was Madrid in October 1991, which transformed the whole process of Arab–Israeli negotiations because, whatever excuses or justifications the Israelis and Arabs wanted to use after Madrid as to why there couldn't be a dialogue, why there couldn't be a negotiation, the one justification they could never use again, and they still can't use it to this day, is that there is nobody at the other end of the table. Madrid shattered that excuse forever.

Both sides might not like what they hear but they are partners. In my judgment, Oslo was the second departure point, particularly in view of what it did for Israelis and Palestinians. Finally, what happened in 2000, even though it did not succeed, that is an effort by the Israeli government of Ehud Barak to negotiate permanent status agreements with both Syria and the Palestinians within a six-month period of one another, boggles the mind in how ambitious and bold an undertaking it really was. Barak's purpose has, in my judgment, reshaped the negotiating landscape in the Arab–Israeli conflict in a way that it is not going to be easily reversed.

It may be the cruelest of paradoxes that the Oslo Process, currently criticized and opposed by both the Israelis and Palestinians, for all of its imperfections, may well provide a point of departure for the foreseeable future for some engagement between Israelis and Palestinians. It is a cruel paradox that eight years after Oslo, when permanent status negotiations and agreement was supposed to be a reality, after events of 2000 on the ground, we may in fact be faced with a return to what is incremental and what is partial. But that won't be enough because in the end Israelis and Palestinians need a strategy ultimately to address the core issues that have fueled their conflict. That strategy, I would argue, needs to have three components. *First*, there will have to be a compelling change in the realities on the ground in terms of Israeli and Palestinian behavior. *Second*, there will have to be a negotiating process that fundamentally cuts to the core of the issues that have fueled their conflict, and it will have to be one that is supported by the Arab states. And, *third*, as naive and foolish as it may appear, there is going to have to be a process of education, and it may be generational, which fundamentally changes the attitudes and images that the Israelis and Palestinians currently have toward one another. And maybe perhaps, one day, if Israelis and Palestinians can find a way to address all of these components, they may succeed in negotiating with one another a lasting and a durable peace.

3

Ending the Conflict: Can the Parties Afford it?

Khalil Shikaki

The failure of the Camp David summit in July 2000 to produce a Framework Agreement on Permanent Status left Palestinians and Israelis in a difficult impasse, dashing Palestinian hopes for an end to the Israeli occupation of Palestinian areas in the West Bank and the Gaza Strip. The eruption of popular and armed confrontations later in September ended a seven-year Oslo process and ushered in a process of violence and radicalization. Both sides have different perceptions of the nature of these two events that came to characterize an end of an era.

The Israelis portrayed these events as involving a generous Israeli offer, a stretched hand, and an unparalleled compromise that was met by Palestinian violent rejection. This violence has been portrayed by Israel as being deliberate and orchestrated and sustained by the Palestinian leadership and the Palestinian security services. This violence, Israel claims, has revealed the true face of Palestinians: they are unwilling to accept Israel and are not capable of making peace with it. Israel has particularly focused on the Palestinian insistence on the "right of return" and sought to portray it as reflecting a Palestinian hidden agenda and real intention, which is to dismantle the State of Israel.

The Palestinian perception is different. In the beginning, when Oslo's Declaration of Principles was signed in 1993, Palestinians expected the peace process to lead to the end of occupation. In the end, Palestinian disillusionment and frustration with the peace process led the public to see Oslo as a cover used by consecutive Israeli governments to colonize the land and transfer Israeli civilians into it, confiscate land to build homes for Jewish settlers, build bypass roads that criss-cross Palestinian territory in a way that make contiguity impossible and prevent the implementation of any national developmental project, thus turning Palestine into more than a hundred small enclaves in a sea of Israeli-controlled territory. In other words, the Palestinians saw the peace process as providing Israel with the means to consolidate, rather than end, occupation.

This chapter examines the causes for the failure of the Palestinian–Israeli peace process, which led to a second Palestinian Intifada, violent confrontations, and a breakdown in a relationship that built up over a seven-year period.

The Failure at Camp David

The Oslo process was not without successes. It transformed the *strategic* environment for Israel and the PLO, leading to the signing of the Israeli–Jordanian peace treaty and the creation of the Palestinian Authority, thus opening the way for improved Palestinian political relations with the US and Europe. Public opinion surveys among Palestinians and Israelis during the period between 1993 and 2000 indicate a transformed *psychological* environment. The two societies supported the process and accepted each other. Willingness to compromise and accept an eventual reconciliation was evident in many areas. Israelis came to recognize the need for the establishment of a Palestinian state and the Palestinians came to recognize the need for the establishment of two states in historic Palestine. Both sides supported many forms of reconciliation, including living in peace and cooperation with open borders, joint economic ventures, and a certain level of political and social normalization. The Oslo process led also to the creation and the institutionalization of an extensive network of legal and political norms that came to govern and organize their relationships. The process affirmed, even if implicitly, the commitment of the two sides to the eventual creation of two political entities. These successes were not sufficient, however, to lead to an agreement on permanent status or prevent the eruption of the second Palestinian Intifada.

Internal Palestinian and Israeli debate about the failure of Camp David and the eruption of the Intifada and violence reveals *three* strands of thought on its causes.

(1) The collapse revealed an existing fundamental clash of interests that diplomacy alone cannot bridge. The Israeli insistence on annexation of vital parts of the West Bank and Arab East Jerusalem, and sovereignty over *al-Haram al-Sharif* (the Temple Mount), and the Palestinian insistence on the return of four million Palestinian refugees to Israel are seen as the two most prominent examples of this unbridgeable clash of interests. In other words, continued conflict, in this view, is seen as inevitable and the best one can hope for is a long term truce or interim agreement. The Camp David summit failed because it went too far; it was too ambitious. This view is

particularly adhered to by right-wing groups in Israel and by Islamists and national opposition within the Palestinian camp.

(2) A second view argues that the failure at Camp David was merely temporary and in fact "technical." Lack of sufficient time, complexity of the issues, misperception, and personality factors have all been mentioned by Palestinian and Israeli negotiators as factors contributing to the failure. In this view, Camp David ushered in significant progress on all issues of permanent status; further negotiations and perhaps another summit would have produced a Framework Agreement. Although this view is not widely shared, senior officials from both sides, with intimate knowledge and involvement in the negotiations, have repeatedly publicized it.

(3) A third view, argued in this chapter, takes a middle road between the two. In this view, the failure of the peace process has been the product of four interacting dynamics: underlying structural difficulties, the open-ended nature of the Oslo agreement, domestic political constraints, and problematic negotiating techniques. In this view, progress has been possible; but it has not been sufficient to sustain a successful process. Indeed, during 2000, and contrary to the expectations of many, Palestinians and Israelis made significant progress on all issues of the permanent settlement including Jerusalem and refugees. Nevertheless, by the time this historic achievement was coming to light, neither side was able to endorse it: Barak was on his way out of office and Arafat and the Palestinian leadership were too weak to endorse it. Public opinion on both sides, enraged by months of violence and mass confrontations, shifted in a very short period to hawkish positions thus greatly reducing their leaders' room for maneuver. The cost of ending the conflict has proven to be too prohibitive for either side to contemplate. Both sides contributed to this outcome.

Structural difficulties

When the Palestinian national movement altered its political national ideology in the mid-1970s, abandoning the slogan of "liberation and return" and adopting the "two-state solution," it failed to fully grasp the implications and the critical requirements of such a fundamental transfor-mation. The transformation itself was motivated by pragmatic considerations. Searching for survival, the PLO, in a preemptive step, sought to capitalize on socioeconomic developments on the inside, and to present itself as a serious potential negotiator in a competition against actors on the outside.

The Palestinian national movement never seriously debated the implica-tions of that change on three issues: the "right of return" as understood up until that point by the refugees; the Palestinian relationship with the "other" state, Israel; and the nature of the Palestinian state itself. The failure to do so was motivated by political calculations: the PLO did not want to lose the support of its largest constituency, the refugees; and it did not want to weaken its negotiating position *vis-à-vis* Israel. Israel, on the other hand, preferred for too long to ignore the Palestinian national movement. When it did finally recognize the PLO and the legitimate political rights of the Palestinians, Israel nonetheless sought to mitigate the consequences of such recognition on all issues vital to the Palestinians: the state, the land, and the people. Israel continued to view the Palestinian entity-state as an Israeli protectorate that must be kept under security control. Disagreement over Palestine's sovereignty, its control over its own borders, its military capability, and its external security and foreign policy poisoned relations between the two sides. On the issue of land, Israel never ceased settlement activities believing that occupied Palestinian territory were war spoils that could be colonized. As the size of the "cake" began to quickly shrink while the two sides negotiated its fate, the overwhelming majority of the Palestinians lost all confidence in the peaceful intentions of Israel. But perhaps it was Israel's failure to treat the Palestinian people with dignity that made reconciliation impossible. It rarely treated them as equal; instead daily suffering and humiliation for the man and women on the street continues unabated.

For the Palestinians, the inability to live up to the requirements of a two-state solution created a barrier threatening to block the fulfillment of their national aspirations. For the Israelis, the inability to treat the Palestinians as people with equal rights led to more hate and violence. The unintended outcome of the deliberate policies of the two sides led to a prolonged political stalemate.

The open-ended nature of Oslo

The open-ended nature of the Oslo agreement postponed for up to six years the resolution of the vital issues of the conflict. As a means to resolve a protracted conflict, Oslo's open-endedness only exacerbated an already existing uncertainty. It meant that neither side would make a full commitment to the peace process. As a result, three dynamics were encouraged. First, both sides wanted to keep their options open, thus leading to an Israeli determination to transfer to the Palestinians as little land as possible, and to a Palestinian unwillingness to completely revise the educational system. Secondly, since the major vital objectives of one or both sides were not achieved during the transitional phase, neither side was willing to completely give up its negotiating assets, including the ability to inflict violence, pain, and suffering. Thirdly, since "real" negotiations have not even started, both sides sought to improve their negotiating positions. Since

Israel was stronger and controlled the land in question, its settlement policy proved most effective in prejudicing final status negotiations.

Creating "facts on the ground" poisoned Palestinian–Israeli relations, an outcome that was the exact opposite to the logic of transitionalism. That logic was simple: the transitional process was expected to transform the political and psychological environment, making possible the resolution of very difficult problems. However, by the time the two sides met at Camp David, the size of the settlements' population had doubled in comparison to what it was when the Oslo process began. Israelis were now more determined than ever to safeguard and develop their settlement enterprise, while Palestinians were more determined to oppose it.

The triumph of domestic political constraints

Three domestic factors proved instrumental in constraining the abilities of the two sides to make the necessary compromises for peace. First, the peace process continued to suffer from a lack of legitimacy in the eyes of a significant sector of the population on both sides. Israeli settlers and extreme right-wing elements opposed it and resorted to violence to stop it, culminating in the assassination of the Israeli Prime Minister, Yitzhak Rabin. This lack of consensus influenced the Israeli leadership's willingness to confront the settlers; in fact, it forced that leadership to seek to appease the settlers in order to gain their approval. On the Palestinian side, the Islamists and the national opposition refused to recognize the legitimacy of the peace process or the Palestinian Authority it created. The Palestinian opposition resorted to violence against Israelis in search for means to bring an end to the peace process. The PA, perceiving a lack of legitimacy, was constrained in its ability to confront the opposition for fear of internal strife.

Second, neither side was able to put together a stable peace coalition capable of governing and at the same time of making difficult compromises. The Israeli labor government lost the critical 1996 elections just as the components of the Interim Agreement were being put in place. Right-wing governments were not willing to implement Israel's commitments and in fact sought to reverse the process by accelerating the pace of settlement expansion. Ehud Barak invited the Shas religious party and a centrist Russian immigrants party to join his left-wing government in the second half of 1999, believing that he could count on them to support his peace policy. But he lost both parties even before reaching Camp David in mid-2000. Internal political and personal rivalries among Arafat's senior colleagues, particularly Mahmud Abbas (Abu Mazin) and Ahmad Qurie (Abu Ala) left him almost alone at Camp David.

Third, public opinion on both sides remained reluctant to accept the painful compromises required for a lasting and comprehensive peace.

Despite the tremendous progress in public attitudes among Israelis and Palestinians regarding many peace related issues, some positions remained almost unchanged. As the two leaderships were meeting at Camp David, neither public was willing to entertain compromise on the issues of Jerusalem or refugees. Indeed, these two particular issues of final status negotiations remained outside public discourse throughout the seven years of the interim period between 1993 and 2000. It is not surprising then that little progress in Camp David negotiations was registered on these two issues.

Flawed negotiating techniques

The Oslo negotiating framework suffered from a serious flaw. It demanded that the Palestinians pay a price for peace twice: once for admission to the negotiating table, and once again for reaching a peace agreement. The Palestinians conceded only to the first price, believing that they were simply being asked to make their peace-making concessions in advance. To them, the price for making peace has been the recognition of the state of Israel in 78 percent of their homeland and the establishment of a Palestinian state in the remaining 22 percent, a price they have paid long before sitting at the final status negotiations. The Israelis, however, saw this Palestinian concession as a precondition for talking to the Palestinians. When the Palestinians at Camp David rejected an Israeli offer that failed to meet Palestinian expectations, Israelis began to doubt Palestinian peace intentions.

At Camp David, once serious final status negotiations started, Israel demanded the annexation of several settlement blocs, the imposition of security arrangements that would have allowed Israeli military forces to "enter" the state of Palestine during times of Israeli-declared "emergencies," and the imposition of severe political restrictions on Palestinian sovereignty, including the Israeli right to freely use Palestinian airspace. Moreover, Israel refused to recognize Palestinian sovereignty over the Muslim holy place of *al-Haram al-Sharif* in Jerusalem and rejected the recognition of the refugees' right of return. While the Palestinians were willing to accept some of those Israeli demands, if proper *quid pro quos* were offered, they could not renounce sovereignty over *al-Haram* or the right of return.

Specifically, Israel offered to end its occupation on 75 percent of the Palestinian territory leaving 12 percent of the West Bank under Israeli sovereignty and 13 percent under Israeli military control for an indefinite period of time. Israel refused to accept the notion of an equal exchange of territory. The Palestinian state could not have territorial contiguity under the Israeli proposal, as Israel would annex or have access to settlements (such as Ariel) deep inside the West Bank heartland. With regard to

Jerusalem, the Israeli initial offer included demands for Israeli sovereignty over Islam's second holiest place on earth, *al-Haram al-Sharif* (Noble Sanctuary) with its two mosques that were built some 1,300 years ago, an Israeli right to build a Jewish synagogue in *al-Haram*, and the right of Jews to pray inside *al-Haram*. Israel may have later dropped or toned down the second and third demands. Occupied East Jerusalem was to remain under Israeli sovereignty, except for unspecified areas in the northern part of the city which were supposed to come under Palestinian sovereignty or self-rule; other Palestinian areas in the occupied Eastern part were to be given self-rule under Israeli sovereignty. With regard to refugees, Israel refused to acknowledge its role and responsibility in creating the refugee problem; refused to acknowledge the right of return; and refused to take full responsibility for refugee compensation. Israel also refused to turn over to the Palestinian side the documents and the value of the assets controlled by the Israeli Absentee Property Authority. On security arrangements, Israel demanded full demilitarization of the Palestinian state, the continued deployment of its military in the Jordan Valley for an unlimited period of time, and the right to send its full army into the territory of the Palestinian state whenever the government of Israel declared an emergency.

The Palestinians insisted on an Israeli withdrawal to the 1967 borders but were willing, nonetheless, to accept of the notion of an equal territorial "exchange" or "swap" within parameters that would not threaten the contiguity of the state or disenfranchise its citizens. On Jerusalem, the Palestinians agreed to allow the Jewish settlements in Arab East Jerusalem, the "Wailing Wall," and the Jewish Quarter of the Old City to come under Israeli sovereignty as part of the territorial exchange. On refugees, the Palestinian position accepted the principle that the Palestinian state would become home to all refugees choosing to exercise the right of return in Palestine and that the implementation of the "right of return" in Israel proper would take into account the realities and sovereignty of the Jewish state. On security, the Palestinians accepted the principle that the State of Palestine would not possess major weapon systems and that Israeli armed forces would withdraw gradually from the Jordan Valley, and that an international force would be deployed in the Valley.

A second flaw in the negotiating technique was Israel's insistence on the phased implementation of its obligations under the Interim Agreement. Gradually, Israel lost any incentive to implement those obligations, such as the "further redeployments," the release of prisoners, the return of displaced persons, and other obligations. Israeli leaders began to view these as "assets" Israel needed as part of expected trade-offs in the final status negotiations. The implementation of these Israeli interim commitments always provided the two sides with a much-needed time to reach a permanent agreement and a cushion to fall back on in case of failure in the final status talks. Throughout 2000, Israeli Prime Minister Ehud Barak refused to implement the so called "third redeployment" or to release Palestinian prisoners, hoping to use these two issues as a leverage in the ongoing permanent status negotiations.

A Second Palestinian Intifada

The Palestinian public negatively perceived the Israeli proposals presented at Camp David. Israel's public presentation of its position as "take it or leave it" deepened Palestinian despair and disbelief in the ability of the peace process to yield results culminating in the end of occupation and establishment of a sovereign independent state.

The Israeli demands for sovereignty over *al-Haram*, the right to build a synagogue, and praying rights heightened Palestinian public fear of Israel intentions and designs for *al-Haram*. Continued debate between mainstream and extreme religious and political groups in Israel about a possible location for the synagogue in the plateau of *al-Haram* only fueled the Palestinian's perception regarding the future of their sacred religious place. Ariel Sharon's visit to *al-Haram* was seen by the public as further evidence of Israel's real intentions to unilaterally implement its designs over *al-Haram*. It provoked an angry and frightened response.

The use of excessive force by the Israeli police against demonstrations of unarmed civilians in *al-Haram* and elsewhere in the West Bank and the Gaza Strip led to deaths and the injury of thousands. The Israeli policy of massive and excessive use of force coupled with an extensive system of collective punishment, closures and siege, destruction of homes, agricultural land, factories, and other property helped to sustain the Intifada.

While expressing Palestinian frustration with the failure of the peace process and affirming Palestinian demands for an end to occupation and settlement construction and expansion, the Intifada led also to several unintended consequences that impact on the ability of the two sides to revive the peace process. Many PA institutions failed to function under the pressure generated by the Israeli restrictions. The failure of the peace process, coupled with the failure of PA institutions to deliver services to the civilian population, led to serious questioning of PA legitimacy.

Other sources of legitimacy began to surface. Fatah, claiming "revolutionary legitimacy," Hamas, claiming "Islamic legitimacy," and the PLO, claiming "national legitimacy," began to assert themselves at the expense of the PA. The challenge to PA's legitimacy could lead to its collapse if and when Israel begins to seriously threaten its infrastructure and when the PA runs out of financial resources. The ability of the PA to generate revenues has been severely restricted as a result of rising unemployment and the halt to economic activity due to closures and siege. One of the other outcomes of the Intifada has been the negative impact it had on Palestinian and Israeli public opinion. Each society perceived the action of the other as highly threatening. This mutual threat perception elicited highly hostile responses, leading, among Palestinians, to a rise in support for armed attacks against Israelis, including civilians. In June 2001, support for attacks against Israeli civilians, including suicide attacks, soared to more than 70 percent. When compared to the level of support to such attacks in 1996, which stood then at 20 percent, one can see the difference generated by the Intifada and the failure of the peace process. Similarly, more than 80 percent of the Israeli public supported the use of massive military force against the Palestinians and in fact wanted the imposition of even more severe collective punishment measures. The two publics show less willingness than ever to compromise on the difficult issues of refugees and Jerusalem.

What Way Out?

The success of the Israelis and Palestinians in moving the peace process forward in significant ways at the Taba talks in January 2001 indicates that progress was attainable despite the breakdown in the relationship between the two sides. The results of these talks show that the ultimate Palestinian objective is not to deny or threaten the existence, peace, or security of the Jewish state. Palestinians want an independent state in the West Bank and Gaza, and to live in peace and cooperation with Israel. This has been the paramount Palestinian national objective since the mid-1970s and has not changed since. It has been enshrined in the Algiers' PNC 1988 resolution and cemented by the PNC annulment of the PLO charter since Oslo. The Palestinian state, as agreed by the two sides at the Taba talks, would pose no threat to any of its neighbors and would rely on international guarantees and good neighborly relations for its security and the safety of its citizens. Palestinian–Israeli success at the Taba talks indicate that the two sides believe that achieving a permanent peace, putting an end to the conflict, and starting the process of reconciliation is an achievable goal that can be obtained now, not later.

Palestinians intend to build a state that would, just like Israel, welcome all its Diaspora, all those Palestinians who aspire to self-determination, peace, and security in a state of their own. This state would particularly welcome all those Palestinians who suffered most from the historic conflict and lived in poverty and dispossession in refugee camps. Palestinian demands for an Israeli recognition of the principle of the refugees' right of return to their homes is not meant to threaten or undermine the national identity or security of the state of Israel. To the contrary, it seeks to close the file on the historic conflict and thus assure all Israelis of their future and the future of their state.

Israeli refusal to implement the main clauses of Oslo (by refusing to withdraw from Palestinian areas and by expanding the settlement process) has confronted the Palestinians with grave threats to their security, existence and aspiration for freedom and independence, leading to desperation and disillusionment among the majority of Palestinians. Continual confrontation and bloodshed have demonstrated that neither violence nor military campaigns can bring about peace. Palestinians do want to put an end to the violence, as they are the ones who suffer the most from it.

The path to peace starts by a return to cooperation between the two sides, full implementation of previous agreements under international monitoring and supervision, cessation of all settlement activities in occupied Palestinian land, and a return to the negotiating table with the aim of putting an end to the conflict by signing and fully implementing a permanent peace agreement.

Specifically, the two sides need to embrace a package of stabilization that would contain three elements: reduction of threat perception, restoration of confidence in the peace process, and a mechanism for monitoring and verification. Once in place, the two sides can then return to final status negotiations.

Reducing threat perception

The rise in support for violence and military strikes among Israeli and Palestinian publics can only be stabilized by ending violence and freezing settlement expansion. If achieved, stabilization makes people willing to take risks and accept compromises for the sake of peace.

Restoring confidence in the peace process

As in the past, the implementation of the remaining items in the Interim Agreement can restore confidence in the peace process and make people more willing to support negotiations and oppose violence.

Verify intentions through an international role

The deployment of monitors to verify implementation of the agreement can give each side confidence that the other is serious about respecting its obligations and the commitments enshrined in signed agreements.

4

Domestic Israeli Politics and the Conflict

Abraham Diskin

A Personal Note

Whenever I think about the Arab–Israeli conflict, a family story about the 1929 riots in Jerusalem comes to mind. At that time, my father, who was very young, worked in my grandfather's office in the old commercial area of Jerusalem. This is the area, at a top of a hill, located between the walls of the Old City and the Jaffa Road. Almost every day when I drive to the Hebrew University on Mount Scopus, I go through that area, on the imaginary borderline between the Arab and Jewish parts of Jerusalem.

When my father heard Arab cries "Atbakh-al-Yahud" (slaughter the Jews), he went out, weaponed with the curiosity of a young and naive person, to find out what was going on. After a few hours the riots came to an end. Everybody went home, but my father disappeared. "The worst has happened," everybody thought. Then came the telephone call. There were not too many telephones in Jerusalem at that time, but the story tells that "our" telephone number was 23. On the other side of the line was no other than the most extreme religious and political leader of the Arab community in Palestine, the initiator of the riots, Haj Amin al Husseini. He came from an affluent family that had several business ties with the Jewish community. The Husseinis also had business ties with my grandfather. Haj Amin spoke Arabic: "your son is in my hands," he said. "Don't worry, I guarantee that he won't lose a single hair on his head." "Tomorrow morning, he will return home, accompanied by my bodyguards." He kept his promise, and thus I can claim that, in a way, I owe my life to Haj Amin, the man who directly and indirectly was responsible for the violent deaths of so many Jews and Arabs in Palestine.

I remember this story because of many personal emotional reasons, but I also believe that it reflects the fact that the Palestinian–Israeli conflict is characterized by contradictions, many of which continue to dictate the political agenda of the Middle East and the whole world. In the following pages some of these contradictions will be discussed.

The Micro-political Level

There are four basic concepts that characterize the nature of the Israeli political system.

One characteristic – *the quest for security* – is quite unique to Israel and can hardly be found in other Western democracies. It has to do with the fact that Israel has faced existential threats ever since its establishment. At times, all of its neighbors called for its elimination. Today, such threats are less frequent, but unfortunately they may express even greater dangers because of a number of developments such as the proliferation of mass-destruction weapons. I regret that even one of the participants at the Colgate conference consistently calls for the elimination of the State of Israel. At the same time, I respect him for his sincerity. The intention, he is ready to admit, is shared by others, who are not as sincere, and who prefer to hide their true beliefs behind a peaceful mask. The existential security issue is not only national. It is also personal, given, among other reasons, the continuing terrorist attacks against Israeli citizens and Jews outside Israel. The present war of attrition, which was launched against Israel in late September 2000, is apparently based on the assumption that the personal threats to the security of Israelis will have national consequences.

Another important feature of the Israeli polity is the *quest for peace*. For most Western democracies peaceful relations with neighboring countries and other nations is a fact, not a problem. In the Israeli case, while most politicians and their followers support the desire for "peace and security," some may question whether peace is possible at all or whether the desire for peace (and the "costs" of peace) contradicts security needs.

In a number of most important constitutional norms, including several basic laws and the Declaration of Independence, Israel is depicted as a "democratic-Jewish" state. The democratic nature and the Jewish nature of the State of Israel are two other basic features of Israel. Many Arabs claim that the Jewish nature of Israel contradicts its democratic nature. A number of model stable democracies do mention in their laws the national nature of the system. It is interesting to explore what Israeli citizens reflect on this issue. Today, many Israelis argue that Israel is a Jewish-Democratic state, but that it is also a "state of all of its citizens." Are we dealing here with slogans, a real problem, or a contradiction?

In a public opinion poll conducted prior to the 1999 general elections, respondents were asked several questions about such issues: 995 citizens, who represent the whole population (including non-Jews), were interviewed face-to-face between April 29 and May 5. Four statements to which the respondents were asked to react were:

1. It is important that the government will make any effort possible in order to achieve peace (hereafter "Peace");
2. It is important that the government will make any effort possible in order to guarantee security (hereafter "Security");
3. It is important that the government will make any effort possible in order to preserve the Jewish nature of the state of Israel (hereafter "Jewish nature");
4. It is important that the government will make any effort possible in order to preserve the democratic nature of the state of Israel (hereafter "Democratic nature").

Table 4.1 depicts the distribution of answers of the respondents, who could "absolutely agree" (1), "agree" (2), "maybe agree" (3), "disagree" (4), or "absolutely disagree" (5).

Table 4.1 Public positions concerning statements on peace, security, the Jewish nature and the democratic nature of the State of Israel

	N	1	2	3	4	5	Mean
Peace	988	63.7%	27.0%	5.4%	2.6%	1.3%	1.51
Security	979	80.4%	15.2%	2.8%	0.7%	0.9%	1.27
Jewish Nature	989	39.2%	29.7%	14.2%	8.5%	8.4%	2.17
Democratic nature	985	91.2%	15.6%	2.1%	0.4%	0.7%	1.24

It is evident that Israeli citizens support very strongly all four positions. In fact, 61 percent of the respondents either "agreed" or "absolutely agreed" with all the statements. This is quite surprising given the fact the only 69 percent supported the "Jewish nature" statement and given the possible contradictions between some of the statements.

In order to compare different groups of respondents the absolute value of the difference between the mean responds of the groups was divided by 4 (the maximal difference possible). The result is a set of "polarization" coefficients. The maximal polarization, 1, is achieved when all the members of one group "absolutely agree" with a given statement, while all the members of the other group "absolutely disagree" with the same statement. The minimal polarization, 0, is achieved when the mean respond of the two examined group is identical. Table 4.2 represents the level of polarization between Jewish respondents and Arab respondents, and the level of polarization between Netanyahu supporters and Barak supporters in the 1999 elections.

Table 4.2 The Jewish–Arab polarization and the Netanyahu followers–Barak followers' polarization concerning statements on peace, security, the Jewish nature, and the democratic nature of the State of Israel

	Jewish–Arab polarization	Netanyahu followers–Barak followers polarization
Peace	0.12	0.15
Security	0.31	0.02
Jewish Nature	0.65	0.27
Democratic nature	0.11	0.08

It seems clear that the polarization between "right-wingers" (Netanyahu supporters) and "left-wingers" (Barak supporters) tend to be marginal. The only issue where one finds a more considerable polarization between these two groups of voters is the question of the "Jewish nature" of Israel. It seems that many interpreted this statement in religious terms. Hence, secular Jews tended in some cases not to agree. The share of religious Jews among Netanyahu supporters is higher than among Barak supporters. Polarization between Jews and Arab voters tends to be more significant. It is most prominent as far as the "Jewish nature" of the state is concerned. It is also evident concerning the security issue. This results from the fact that Israeli Arabs do not perceive "other" Arabs as threatening as they are perceived by most of the Jewish citizens.

In fact, this question of "enemy image" seems crucial in Israeli politics, in spite of the relatively minimal polarization between "hawks" and "doves." Jewish–Arab polarization on the statement "the Palestinians would have wanted to destroy Israel had they had the chance to do so" was at a level of 0.61 prior to the 1996 elections and 0.42 prior to the 1999 elections. Now it is at its peak, but even before the 1999 elections only 20 percent of all the respondents (including Arabs) "disagreed," 20 percent hesitated and approximately 60 percent either "agreed" or "absolutely agreed."

It should also be noted that when people are asked to rank themselves on a Left–Right dimension, more people identify with either the Right or the Left on questions related to the Arab–Israel conflict then those identifying with one of the camps on questions related to social and economic policies. Obviously, this puts Israel in a unique position compared with other Western democracies. It is also important to note that when concrete questions, such as specific policies or specific territories are concerned, the polarization between left-wingers and right-wingers tends to grow.

In the public opinion poll mentioned above, the respondents were asked to specify whether they "agreed" to the following statements:

1. Within the framework of a peace agreement with the Palestinians, Israel should evacuate settlements (hereafter "Settlements").
2. Within the framework of a peace agreement with Syria, Israel should agree to full withdrawal from the Golan Heights (hereafter "Golan").
3. Within the framework of a peace agreement with the Palestinians, Israel should give up the Jordan Valley (hereafter "Jordan Valley").
4. Within the framework of a peace agreement with the Palestinians, Israel should agree to the partition of Jerusalem (hereafter "Jerusalem").

Public stands on concrete issues tend to be far less stable than the stands on more general questions. The general rule is that the public tends to follow the government (and to change positions) whenever the government (be it a dovish or a hawkish government) makes a dramatic move on questions of war and peace. Thus, only a slight minority supported full evacuation of the Sinai Peninsula prior to the Begin–Sadat Camp David agreement. After the 1978 agreement, a clear majority, which included many right-wingers, supported it. It should be remembered that the territories returned to Egypt consist of 90 percent of all the territories occupied by Israel in the 1967 Six Day War. Likewise, only a few supported the penetration to Lebanon prior to the "Peace for Galilee" operation of 1982. A clear majority, which included many left-wingers, supported the government once the war in Lebanon started. Prior to the first Oslo agreement (September 1993), a vast majority of Israelis objected to the idea of any form of negotiations with the PLO, which was commonly perceived as an extreme terrorist organization affiliated with the most extreme Arab regimes such as Saddam Hussein's Iraq. Only a minority supported such stands in the following years.

The distribution of stands depicted in table 4.3 below reflects the situation prior to the 1999 elections. Positions during the Arafat–Barak Camp David talks tended to be far more dovish. After the failure of the talks, and following the outbreak of Palestinian violence in late September 2000, many returned to views more hawkish than those depicted in table 4.3.

In general, one may claim that a majority of Israelis supports withdrawal from most of the territories – and even the evacuation of at least some of the settlements – but only a minority supports full withdrawal from the Golan Heights and the Jordan Valley. There is also a very clear objection to the idea of partition of Jerusalem.

Table 4.3 Public positions concerning statements on Settlements, the Golan Heights, the Jordan Valley, and the Partition of Jerusalem

	1	2	3	4	5	Mean
Settlements	31.6%	21.2%	17.0%	16.0%	14.2%	2.60
Golan	9.2%	7.8%	17.5%	28.7%	36.8%	3.76
Jordan Valley	7.4%	8.2%	16.3%	36.5%	31.6%	3.77
Jerusalem	9.6%	8.4%	11.0%	19.4%	51.6%	3.95

Table 4.4 The Jewish–Arab polarization and the Netanyaku followers–Barak followers polarization concerning statements on Settlements, the Golan Heights, the Jordan Valley, and the Partition of Jerusalem

	Jewish–Arab polarization	Netanyahu followers–Barak followers polarization
Settlements	0.67	0.55
Golan	0.63	0.33
Jordan Valley	0.63	0.21
Jerusalem	0.72	0.31

Israeli Arab citizens, unlike most of the Jewish citizens, tend to support very strongly a full withdrawal from all the territories including the Golan Heights, the Jordan Valley and Jerusalem, and the evacuation of the Jewish settlements in the West Bank and the Gaza Strip. Hence, the very clear Arab–Jewish polarization depicted in table 4.4. The sharpest polarization between doves and hawks within the Jewish population concerns the question of settlements. Thus, Netanyahu supporters tended to object to any evacuation of settlements, while Barak supporters tended to accept the idea of evacuation of at least some of the settlements.

The bottom line is that Israelis are very interested in peace. They support the promotion of peace whole-heartedly even when they are "hawks." At the same time Israelis are very anxious about security issues. This is the reason why so many Israelis have deep reservations concerning a full withdrawal from the Golan Heights and the Jordan Valley. These areas are regarded by many as crucial as far as security considerations are concerned. The majority of Israelis believe that the Arab world does stick – at least latently – to its desire to eliminate the State of Israel. This belief characterizes both hawks and doves. The only significant group that deviates from such a tendency consists of Israeli Arabs. As far as specific policies are concerned, there do exist issues – additional to the settlements question – on which one can easily point at evident differences even among Israeli Jews. Nevertheless, as demonstrated above, past surveys prove that dramatic changes in stands on specific policies do occur following dramatic changes in governmental policy.

In a democracy one expects the existence of a strong link between the beliefs held by voters and beliefs held by their leaders. Hereafter the influence of stands on the Arab–Israeli conflict on coalition behavior will be discussed. In addition, it has been proved in a number of surveys that voters attribute priority to issues associated with security and foreign policy in their preference for political parties. Political leaders, who are aware of this fact, respond adequately not only because of their own positions, but also because of this awareness.

In a public opinion poll conducted prior to the 1996 elections 1,064 citizens, who represent the whole population (including non-Jews), were interviewed face-to-face between May 7 and May 17. The respondents were asked the following question: "What, in your opinion, is the main reason why voters prefer a specific political party in general elections?" Table 4.5 compares the answers of Jewish and Arab voters.

Table 4.5 Reasons for support of political parties given by Jewish and Arab voters prior to the 1996 general election (in percentages)

Reason of support	Jewish voters	Arab voters	Total
Security and Foreign policy issues	53	22	48
Party stands on other issues	6	19	8
Belief in party leaders	14	21	15
"The party represents people like me"	18	33	20
Other reasons	9	5	9
N	848	178	1026

The findings of table 4.5, as well as findings of similar investigations conducted in the last two decades, demonstrate the supreme influence of "security and foreign policy issues" on voting behavior. Although the results differed over time, the conflict between Israel and its neighbors, and especially the Israeli–Palestinian conflict, always emerged as the most prominent reason for partisan affiliation. Findings concerning the Arab population are different. It seems that many Arab voters tend to support not only "dovish," but especially "Arab" parties. This is apparently taken for granted by most of them. Hence, the importance of parties that represent "people like me" to Arab respondents. It is also interesting to note that "security and foreign policy issues" tend to be more important for right-wing voters then for left-wingers. In the survey discussed here, 53 percent of Netanyahu supporters mentioned these issues as their main reason for party selection, compared with only 43 percent of Peres supporters.

The Macro-political Level

In order to understand the macro-political level, it seems that one must concentrate on the quite complicated Israeli party system. Figure 4.1 depicts the party system following the 1999 Knesset elections. It should be noted that a number of changes have taken place since the elections. These changes do influence political tactics, but they are not as crucial as far as the general political tendencies are concerned.

The background to the 1999 elections was the negotiations between Netanyahu's government and the Palestinian Authority. The most hawkish elements in Netanyahu's government – especially the NRP – were not satisfied with the way these were proceeding. They suspected that Netanyahu was about to make concessions, which were regarded by them as exaggerated. Once they decided to defect from the coalition, the government lost its majority in the Knesset and early elections seemed inevitable. Netanyahu lost the Prime-Ministirial elections to Barak, but the right-wing parties continued to control half of the Knesset seats, in spite of Likud's losses. The election of the Labor (One Israel) candidate as Prime Minister became possible because of sharp criticism of Netanyahu's personality, and probably also because Barak, a former chief of staff of the Israeli Defense Forces, seemed to be hawkish enough for voters floating between left and right.

Six of the 15 political parties, which won representation in the 1999 elections, should be regarded as "main-stream parties." These political parties may be placed on an uni-dimensional model. They differ from European parties in that in Israel they should be placed according to the position of the parties regarding the Arab–Israeli conflict. The "main-stream" parties are depicted in the centerline of figure 4.1. These parties combined controlled only 68 of the 120 Knesset seats. Other parties are mainly "sectarian" parties. The stands of "sectarian" parties on the Arab–Israeli conflict are not latent, but their main goal is to represent different social groups. Thus, there are "religious" parties, "Arab" parties, and "Russian" immigrants' parties. The "central parties" depicted in figure 4.1 are political parties that would have joined Barak in almost any coalition formed by him following the 1999 elections. Conversely, "third circle" parties are those, the participation of which in any coalition formed by Barak seemed almost impossible. "Second circle" parties are those that would have participated in a Barak coalition under certain circumstances.

Barak formed an "impossible" coalition with a very wide ideological range. The most dovish party in his cabinet was Meretz – a party that also expressed very extreme anti-clerical positions. The most hawkish party in his cabinet was the NRP. In fact, all three religious parties – that had never

Figure 14.1   The party system following the May 17, 199? Knesset Elections

Opposition Parties in the Outgoing Knesset (60)			Coalition Parties in the Outgoing Knesset (60)		
			"Russian Parties"		"National Right"
Balad (2)		Shinui (6)	Yisrael Ba'Alya (6)	Israel our Home (4)	
Hadash (3)	*Meretz (10)*	*One Israel (26)*	*Center Party (6)*	*Likud (19)*	*National Unity (4)*
Ra'am (5)		Am Ehad (2)	Shas (17)	Yehadut Ha'Thora (5)	NRP (5)
"Arab" Parties	Anti-clerical Parties		Religious Parties		

"Central Circle"	"Second Circle"	"Third Circle"	*"Main Dimension" Parties*

gained such a wide representation in any previous elections – became members of Barak's coalition. It was clear that once the government made a significant move on any issue, some of its members would find it impossible to remain in the coalition.

Barak seemed anxious to reach a "comprehensive peace." He declared his intention to achieve this goal "within a year." His policies were attacked more than once, even by more dovish members of the Labor party and Meretz (e.g. Shimon Peres and Yossi Sarid). He crossed all the previously known "red lines" in his negotiations with the Syrians and with the Palestinians, but failed. Many criticize Barak for having a "zigzag" policy on many issues. There is more than a grain of truth in such criticism. Nevertheless, the only policy issue on which Barak remained very consistent was the Arab–Israeli conflict. Some criticize Barak for declaring his readiness to make concessions without implementing such inclinations. Given the fact that under Barak Israel withdrew its forces from Lebanon, and given the deep involvement of the American administration and President Clinton himself in the negotiations, there is not much ground to such criticism.

The final blow to Barak's government came with the Camp David talks with the Palestinians (July 2000). All the "right-wingers" of the coalition decided to defect, leaving Barak with a formal support of only 30 Knesset members.

The 2001 Elections

With the collapse of the Israeli–Palestinian negotiations in spite of Barak's concessions, and with the wave of violence initiated by the Palestinians two months later, the results of the February 6, 2001 elections of the Prime Minister seemed inevitable. The lowest turnout in Israel's history was recorded (62%). Out of the valid voters only 38 percent supported Barak. The full results of the 2001 elections are compared with the 1999 Prime Ministerial elections in table 4.6 below.

Table 4.6 The 1999 and the 2001 Prime Ministerial Elections

17 May 1999			*6 February 2001*		
Eligible Voters	4,285,428		Eligible Voters	4,504,769	
Voters	3,372,952	(78.7%)	Voters	2,805,938	(62.3%)
Valid votes	3,193,494	(94.7%)	Valid votes	2,722,021	(97.0%)
Invalid votes	179,458	(5.3%)	Invalid votes	83,917	(3.0%)
Candidate	*Number Votes*	*Percentage*	*Candidate*	*Number Votes*	*Percentage*
Ehud Barak	1,791,020	56.1	Ehud Barak	1,023,944	37.6
Benjamin Netanyahu	1,402,474	43.9	Ariel Sharon	1,698,077	62.4

It seems that the elected Prime Minister did not have many difficulties in forming a new "national unity" government. The Sharon coalition government included seven party lists, with a total of 72 of the 120 parliamentary seats. The three largest parties in the parliament were included – One Israel (23 MPs), Likud (19), and Shas (17) – along with the merged National Unity–Israel Our Home (7), Yisrael Ba'Aliyah (4), and Am Ehad (2). The vote of investiture was supported by these 72 MPs and opposed by 21, with 27 abstaining. Within the first month of the new government, the 5 MPs of the Yehadut Ha'Torah party and a single member of the Centre Party joined the coalition, raising its majority to 78 MPs. The parliamentary opposition is to the left of the government coalition (the Arab parties and Meretz), in the middle (Shinui and the Center), and on the religious right (National Religious).

The new government includes three women (out of a total of 26 ministers), the largest number ever, and one Arab (Druze) for the very first time. This government can survive for no longer than two and a half years. The reason is that the next parliamentary elections are scheduled for November 2003 (notwithstanding Barak's resignation and the election of Sharon).

On the same day that the new government was sworn in, the Israeli parliament passed a bill that abolished the separate election of the Prime Minister and returned the country to a pure parliamentary form of government. This new electoral and political system will go into effect with the next scheduled elections.

The developments narrowed in many ways not only the polarization between the different political camps on both the micro and the macro political levels, but also the difference between Israeli voters and Israel politicians. Everybody, including many of the more extreme members of Sharon's government, willingly accept now the establishment of a Palestinian state. At the same time only a small percentage continue to believe that "real" peace is achievable. The Palestinians have an opportunity to gain not only an independent state, but also most of the territories that would be handed to them by a relatively "hawkish" government.

Abba Eban used to say about the Palestinians that they "never miss an opportunity to miss an opportunity." The question now is whether a retreat from the Palestinian policies of July and September 2000 is possible or whether another missed opportunity should be expected.

A Concluding Personal Note

In 1967 I was even younger than my father in 1929. Ever since the Six Day War I have believed that a Palestinian State should be established. Several months before Prime Minister Eshkol's death, I even had the opportunity to ask him about it in an event that took place at the Hebrew University. "Young man," Prime Minister Eshkol answered in Yiddish, "I wish I could do what you ask me to do."

I strongly believe that the establishment of a Palestinian State – under the most generous conditions possible – serves the interests of Israelis and Palestinians alike. Jews and Arabs are destined to share this tortured ancient piece of land. In principle, I am confident that the better is the situation for one of the communities, the better it is for its twin community.

At the same time, I must admit that, like most Israelis, I do not believe that a real peace is possible in the coming decades. An agreement can be reached and should be desired, but the depth of the hostility toward Israel leaves the goal of a "real" peace – in which one gives up violence as well as the dream to eliminate the other – in the hands of future generations.

The Arab–Israeli conflict in general and the Palestinian–Israeli conflict in particular remind me of a famous biblical story. Two prophets, Hannaniah, the son of Azur, and Jeremiah, the son of Hilkiah, held a public debate. Nebuchadnezzar, the king of Babylon had just exiled the king of Judea. The question about which the prophets argue is when peace will return. Hannaniah claims that peace will come within two years. "Amen, the Lord do so," responds Jeremiah. But he does not believe in an instant peace. "True prophets," says Jeremiah, "are those whose prophecies are about war, evil and pestilence." "Peace will come," he continues, "but it will take seventy years, not two."

References (Data supplied by the secretary of the government of Israel)

Diskin, A. "Israel – Political Data and National Issues 1991–2000," *European Journal of Political Research: Political Data Yearbook*, Dordrecht: Kluwer, 1992–2001.

—— "The New Political System of Israel," *Government and Opposition*, 34 (4) (Autumn 1999): 498–515.

——, *Jerusalem's Last Days: Guidelines for Examining the New Israeli Democracy*, Jerusalem: The Floersheimer Institute for Policy Studies, 2001.

Diskin, A. and Hazan, R. Y., "The 2001 Prime-Ministirial Elections in Israel," *Electoral Studies* (forthcoming).

Divrei Ha'Knesset, Jerusalem: The Knesset, 1999, 2000 (Official Knesset Records in Hebrew).

Ha'aretz (2000–2001, daily newspaper, Hebrew).

Hazan, R. Y. and Diskin, A. 2000. "The 1999 Knesset and prime ministerial elections in Israel," *Electoral Studies* 19 (4): 628–37.

Israel's Government Yearbook 5760 (2000), Jerusalem: The Government of Israel (Hebrew).

Jerusalem Post (2000–2001, daily newspaper).

Jerusalem Report (2000–2001, weekly magazine).

Who's Who in the 15th Knesset, Jerusalem: The Knesset, 1999 (Hebrew).

The following websites have been used to gather information.
www.knesset.gov.il (Knesset); www.pmo.gov.il (Prime Minister's Office)
www.mfa.gov.il (Ministry of Foreign Affairs); www.meretz.org.il (Meretz Party)
www.oneisrael.co.il (One Israel); www.likud.org.il (Likud Party)
www.hadash.org.il (Hadash Party); www.shinui.org.il (Shinui)
www.haichud-haleumi.org.il (National Unity Party);
www.hamercaz.org.il/ (The Centre Party)
www.Palestine-Net.com

5

Foundering Illusions: The Demise of the Oslo Process

Yossi Ben-Aharon

The PLO

To better understand the reasons for the failure of the Oslo process, a look at the background of the Palestinian partner to the Oslo Accord is necessary.

The Palestinian Authority (PA) that came into being through the Oslo Accords, is the governing organ that was created by the PLO. Its chairman is at one and the same time the chairman of the PLO. Most of the members of the executive body of the PA are members of the Executive Committee of the PLO and many, if not most of the members of the PA Legislative Council, are members of the Palestinian National Council (PNC).

The PLO was established in 1964, reorganized in 1968, and was initially dominated by Arab governments, primarily those of Egypt and Syria. Its declared purpose was the "liberation" of Palestine, which meant the elimination of Israel in its pre-June 1967 borders. At the PNC conference in Algiers in 1988, the Council declared the establishment of a Palestinian state, basing its decision on the UN General Assembly Resolution 181 of 1947, which had then been totally rejected by the Palestinians and by all the Arab states. The Algiers resolution was erroneously interpreted as an indirect, de facto recognition of Israel and the acceptance of the partition of Palestine into two states, one Jewish (Israel) and one Arab (Palestine). In fact, although the Algiers meeting based its declaration of an independent Palestinian state on the UN Partition Resolution of 1947, it made no reference, much less extend any recognition, explicit or implicit, of the State of Israel.

The PLO Covenant and the 1974 Resolutions

The basic, guiding platform, or constitution, of the PLO is the Palestinian National Covenant of 1968.[1] Some 25 out of 33 articles of that covenant called for the elimination of Israel by means of an "armed struggle" and supplanting it with an Arab Palestinian state. At the 21st conference of the PNC in Gaza on April 25, 1996, the articles that contradicted the Oslo Accords were supposedly struck from the covenant. However, the process by which those articles were eliminated was not in accordance with the rules set down by the covenant itself and was therefore questionable, if not altogether invalid.

At its 12th meeting, on June 9, 1974, the PNC decided, after a bitter debate that caused a split in the organization, to adopt political, in addition to military means, to achieve its goals. Paragraphs 2 and 8 of that decision stated, inter alia, that the PLO would "establish the independent, combatant national authority . . . over every part of Palestinian territory that is liberated." Once it is established, "the Palestinian national authority will strive to achieve . . . the aim of completing the liberation of all Palestinian territory . . . " This resolution later became known as the "stage by stage" approach toward the "liberation" of Palestine, meaning, in effect, the elimination of Israel.

At the beginning of February 2001, one hundred Palestinian personalities, including members of the Palestinian Authority's Executive Council and members of the PNC, met in Cairo under the chairmanship of the Speaker of the PNC, Saleem Za'nun. The participants decided to establish a National Independence Authority under the PNC. They passed a number of resolutions, one of which maintained that "the Palestinian National Covenant was still in force, because the PNC had not been convened for the purpose of approving changes in the Covenant and, especially, since the legal committee that should prepare the changes had not been set up."[2]

The Oslo Accords

The basic document in the Accords is the Declaration of Principles on Interim Self-Government Arrangements (DoP),[3] which was signed in Washington on September 13, 1993. The DoP set down the arrangements for the establishment of the Palestinian Council, the transfer of powers and responsibilities to it, its jurisdiction, and the transitional period pending the conclusion of permanent status negotiations. Article VIII empowered the Council to "establish a strong police force, while Israel will continue to carry the responsibility for defending against external threats, as well as the responsibility for overall security of Israelis . . . " Article XV stipulated that disputes "shall be resolved by negotiations" and failing that, the sides could have recourse to a mechanism of conciliation or submit the dispute to arbitration.

More pertinent to the subject of this paper is the exchange of letters between Prime Minister Yitzhak Rabin and PLO Chairman Yasser Arafat, which was attached to the DoP and became an integral part thereof.

In a letter to Rabin dated September 9, 1993, Arafat committed the PLO to "a peaceful resolution of the conflict between the two sides" and declared that "all outstanding issues relating to permanent status will be resolved through negotiations." Arafat stated further that the PLO "renounces the use of terrorism and other acts of violence and will assume responsibility over all PLO elements and personnel in order to assure their compliance, prevent violations and discipline violators." In another letter to Rabin of the same date, Arafat undertook to include in his public statements a call upon the Palestinian people in the West Bank and the Gaza Strip "to take part in the steps leading to the normalization of life, rejecting violence and terrorism, (and) contributing to peace and stability . . . "

The Gaza–Jericho Agreement laid down the mode of implementation of the first stage of the Oslo Accords.[4] Under that agreement and its Security Annex, Israel withdrew its forces from the Gaza Strip and Jericho and the PA was to establish a police force comprising 9,000 men. Israel undertook to release some 5,000 Palestinian prisoners.

The provisions of the Gaza–Jericho Agreement included:

- an undertaking by the PA to give Israel the names of the members of the PA and to inform and gain Israel's consent for any change therein (Art. IV);
- a commitment by the PA not to conduct foreign relations, except in economic, scientific, cultural and educational spheres and foreign aid (Art. VI);
- an undertaking to coordinate legislation with Israel (Art. VII);
- a solemn obligation that the Palestinian Police would be the only body permitted to bear arms and no other organization or person will be permitted to acquire, possess or import firearms or explosives (Art. IX).

Annex I to the Agreement limited the number of firearms possesed by the Police to 7,000 light personal weapons and up to 120 low-caliber machine guns (Art. III); Israeli settlements in the areas transferred to the PA will be under Israeli authority (Art. IV). Two important issues were postponed, to be addressed in the permanent status negotiations: Jerusalem and the Palestinian refugees. Contrary to repeated charges by the Palestinians, there was no undertaking by Israel in the Oslo Accords, or subsequently, with regard to the existence, the expansion, or the establishment of settlements.

Barring foreign relations and external defense and security, the Gaza–Jericho Agreement empowered the PA to conduct its affairs, in the territories under its jurisdiction, in total independence. This principle was subsequently applied over all territories that were transferred to the PA.

The First Cracks

The DoP and the signing ceremony on the White House lawn were universally hailed as a turning point in the history of the century-old Arab–Israel conflict. At the ceremony, the Prime Minister of Israel addressed the Palestinians and said that Israelis and Palestinians "are destined to live together on the same soil in the same land . . . we are today giving peace a chance . . . we wish to open a new chapter . . . of mutual recognition, of good neighborliness, of mutual respect, of understanding."

Addressing the people of Israel, PLO chairman Yasser Arafat said that the two sides "will need more courage and determination to continue the course of building coexistence and peace" and added that "the two peoples are awaiting today this historic hope, and they want to give peace a real chance."

In the course of the Knesset debate on the Oslo Accords, Prime Minister Rabin assured the house that the PLO "had undertaken to enforce the cessation of terror and violent activities on its members and to bring violators of its commitment to justice."[5]

Shortly after the implementation of the Gaza–Jericho Agreement, Rabin sounded optimistic, when he said that "in the six weeks following the implementation of the Gaza–Jericho Agreement, the results are altogether positive, even with regard to security."[6] A month later, four Palestinian terrorists were caught attempting to enter the Gaza Strip in Arafat's entourage illegally.[7]

A few weeks later, Rabin's tone began to change. Referring to the killing of three Israeli soldiers by Palestinians since the Gaza-Jericho implementation, the Prime Minister went on to attach grave significance to the killing of an Israeli civilian near Kissufim, adjacent to the Gaza Strip. Rabin criticized the PA and charged that it was not making a serious effort to deal with the terrorist organizations operating from within PA-held territory. "It does not stand to reason that we continue with the (peace) process without a clear indication that the PA is making a serious effort to quell the groups responsible for terror attacks. This would be the test of the process."[8] Rabin then went on to warn the PA that failure to deal with the terrorist threat will force Israel to draw the consequences.[9] Shortly thereafter, Rabin levelled his criticism at Yasser Arafat personally. If Arafat cannot impose his authority on his people, said Rabin, it is doubtful that he can speak for them.[10]

By the end of January 1995, Rabin had reached the conclusion that the Palestinian terror was a strategic threat. In a cabinet meeting, the Prime Minister reportedly said that "the terror has assumed strategic proportions, because it is threatening the peace process."[11] Foreign Minister Shimon Peres, architect of the Oslo Accords, went a step further. He threatened to halt the negotiations with Arafat if the Palestinian leader would fail to extend his control over the PA-held territory. "If (Arafat) is too weak or unwilling, why should we negotiate with him . . . (and) why should we withdraw from the West Bank?" asked Peres.[12]

In another press interview, the Israeli Prime Minister revealed the agonizing dilemma which he was facing in relation to the peace process with the Palestinians. "Logically, Israelis understand that the time has come to put an end to the conflict in all its aspects. Emotionally, they are not convinced that the PA has the ability, the capacity, or the will to cope with the terror."[13]

Palestinan Violations of the Agreements

Throughout the months and years following the signing of the first Oslo Accord, the Israel government, the media and various research institutes issued a multitude of statements and reports on a wide variety of violations by Yasser Arafat, by the PA, and by individual Palestinians.

Probably the most telling and most serious type of violation were the statements by Yasser Arafat, Chairman of the PA and the PLO, the person who signed all the main agreements between Israel and the PLO/PA, on behalf of the Palestinians.

On September 1, 1993, two weeks before the signing ceremony on the White House lawn, Yasser Arafat made the following statement on Radio Monte Carlo: "The agreement [i.e. the agreement with Israel] will be a basis for an independent Palestinian state in accordance with the Palestine National Council resolution issued in 1974 . . . The PNC resolution issued in 1974 (see above, p. 60), calls for the establishment of a national authority on any part of Palestinian soil from which Israel withdraws or which is liberated."[14]

The 1974 resolution to which Arafat referred, also known as the "phase by phase" resolution, laid down the PNC's "political programme." (See above, p. 60.)

Another type of statement by Yasser Arafat was the often repeated reference to Jihad as a way of achieving Palestinian objectives. Thus, in a speech he delivered in a mosque in Johannesburg on May 10, 1994, he said: "The Jihad will continue . . . You have to understand our main battle is Jerusalem . . . You have to come and to fight a Jihad to liberate Jerusalem, your precious shrine . . . No, it is not their capital. It is our capital."[15] In the course of a speech at a large demonstration of support for Arafat that was organized by the Fatah movement in Gaza, Arafat said: "The Palestinian people are maintaining their Jihad, but the process will continue until one of the Fatah youths or a Palestinian boy will raise the flag over the walls of Jerusalem . . . "[16]

A typical statement by Yasser Arafat is the repeated reference to the extremely controversial issue of the "right of return" of Palestinians to the territory of Palestine in its entirety, including pre-June 1967 Israel. Thus, at a reception in his honor in Gaza, Arafat said: "Be blessed, O Gaza, and celebrate, for your sons are returning after a long celebration. O Gaza, your sons are returning. O Jaffa, O Lod, O Haifa, O Jerusalem, you are returning."[17] All the towns Arafat mentioned, except for Gaza, are in Israel proper.

Another example is Arafat's references to the seventeenth-century Khudaybiyya armistice agreement which was concluded between the city of Mecca and Islam's prophet, Muhammad. In an interview with the *al-Quds* Jerusalem daily, Arafat was asked if he felt he may have made a mistake in concluding the Oslo agreement. Arafat replied: "No . . . no. Allah's messenger Muhammad accepted the al-Khudaybiyya peace treaty . . . "[18] Arafat was thus drawing a parallel between the Oslo agreement and Muhammad's ten-year armistice agreement with the Mecca rulers, which he broke after two years. The clear implication was that the agreement with Israel was of a temporary nature and the Palestinian side can abrogate it whenever it ceased to meet its interests.

On December 13, 1994, the IDF Judge Advocate-General's Assistant for International Law issued a report detailing Palestinian violations of under-takings under the agreements with Israel.[19] Each category of violations was measured against the relevant clause in the various agreements concluded between Israel and the PLO/PA.

Among the more serious violations in the sixteen-page report were: refusal to transfer to Israel Palestinians suspected of involvement in terror attacks; refusal to report to Israel on investigations of terror incidents; non-compliance with the commitment to prevent acts of incitement against Israel; refusal to submit names of policemen who were recruited by the PA; illegal arrest of Israeli citizens by Palestinian police; Palestinian policemen driving (Israeli) stolen vehicles; use of weapons belonging to the Palestinian Police in the course of a terrorist attack in Jerusalem on October 9, 1994; recruitment of former prisoners to the Palestinian Intelligence service; non-compliance with the requirment to prevent infiltrations between Gaza and